For my lovely mum

About the Author

Imogen Lloyd Webber, 30, is a Londoner living and loving the single girl's life. She's almost had as many bosses as boyfriends, but despite multiple mistakes involving mobile phones and men, was still not desperate enough to accept the wonderful opportunity to find true love on ITV1's *Love Island.*

Acknowledgements

The road to publishing a book is a long, winding and sometimes rocky one, and I would like to take this opportunity to say a massive thank you to all my family and friends for helping me along it (I *would* keep hindering my progress by refusing to remove those four-inch heels).

I would also like to say thank you to the team at Summersdale for all their support, in particular Stewart Ferris and the unwavering patience of Jennifer Barclay, Carol Baker, Lucy York, Sarah Herman, Nicky Douglas, Elly Donovan and Robert Melhuish. In addition, thank you to Adrian Weston and Raft for their tireless work on the book's behalf, Veronica Palmieri and Salma Conway for their fabulous SG illustrations and Sam Hiyate for his North American perspective. Anthony Pye-Jeary, Tom Littlechild and everyone at Dewynters have kindly designed the most amazing website.

The Single Girl's Guide would never have been written without some very specific help and I am indebted to: Ele Clow and the Queen's girls; Darryl Samaraweera; Daniel Bee (the best publicist in the world); Wyckoff and his other two angels, Cat and Zoe; Fin; Goli; his Bobness; Wheeler for his semantics; Amanda Johnson; Charlie 'Slashie' Roberts... and LG for sharing his encyclopaedic knowledge on the female species. I would have been lost without the wise words of Caroline Turner, Lucinda, Jess, H, Yael, Diane, Josh, Frances, Julie, Peter, Louise and Theo.

I would not have got here without the encouragement to continue writing over the years from some truly special people in the literary world: Ed Victor; Lizzy Kremer; Marjory Chapman; Toby Eady; Peter James; and Robert Huntington. Thank you so much for making sure I hung on in there and I do so hope to work with you on future projects.

Words cannot express my gratitude to Mummy, Daddy, Nick and Mads.

Alex and Frankie, you are not forgotten.

CONTENTS

GLOSSARY

AG: Attached Girl.

All text no trousers: Phrase used to describe a man who manages to text on a regular basis suggesting you should meet up, but never actually comes up with a date (see also **Clit Teaser**).

AS: Accidental Sex, an **SG**'s version of the one-night stand. Only in exceptional circumstances will an **SG** have a premeditated intention for an encounter to unfold in so unclothed a way as it did, or be under the impression there will be no repeat performances.

Big Duvet: Time spent in one's own abode under one's very own duvet.

BF: Best Friend. Even more precious to you than your shoe collection.

Bunbury: From Oscar Wilde's *The Importance of Being Earnest*; an imaginary friend with a very real role in getting an **SG** out of things she would rather not do.

Cabbage: A cab/taxi; somewhere the in-demand **SG** aims to spend a significant proportion of her time, for then her heels can be high AND she has a chance of making almost all her engagements (see also **Little Black Bus**).

Clit Teaser: An **Object/Distraction** who flirts, but does not follow through.

CL: Conversation List. A thought process or written list prepared for any type of discussion, with a number of questions for you to ask and replies to enquiries likely to be aimed in your direction.

Distraction: A male (or female) an **SG** has her eye on for non-platonic affairs (see also **Object**).

Do dinner off the mirror (verb): To eschew food for **hoovering** cocaine.

EXploitation: Exploitation of skills, knowledge or items obtained from your ex-boyfriends to improve your lifestyle.

GBF: Gay Best Friend.

Genuine Girlfriend: A female friend whom an **SG** can confide in with complete confidence and who absolutely always abides by the 'girls' code' of behaviour, never kissing any of said **SG**'s exes.

Girl Playmate: A female friend who is fantastic to have fun with, but is not necessarily a suitable person to divulge your deepest, darkest secrets to.

Hoover (verb): To snort cocaine.

Horrorscopes: Horoscopes. To be consulted sparingly and with a spoonful of salt.

iPod Icebreaker: A textbook conversation-creating tactic, where a person asks another what the most embarrassing song on his/her iPod is, then reveals theirs.

In harm's way: To be in with a chance of attaining something you desire, most often a new **Distraction/Object** or job.

Joiner: A sanctimonious soul who enjoys organised group activities. If said activities take place outside, **Joiners** will be keen they go ahead whatever the weather.

Kiss (verb): A euphemism which covers all exchange of bodily fluids between an **SG** and a **Distraction/Object**, i.e. anything from literally just kissing someone to full-blown sex.

Kiss and cuddle (verb): Full-blown sex.

Little Black Bus: A taxicab, also known as **Cabbage. SG** prefers to large red variety since she then does not have to trek too far in stilettos.

Metrosexual: A male who spends a vast proportion of his disposable income on his grooming and lifestyle.

NFI (verb): To Not F**king Invite someone to an event; the aim of the game is to be FI'd as much as possible.

Object: As in Object of Affection; a male (or female) an **SG** has her eye on for non-platonic affairs (see also **Distraction**).

Platonic Boyfriend: A male friend of the **SG** whom she does not **kiss**; the 'Boy' version of the **Girl Playmate.**

PMDL: A Promise Much, Deliver Little boy. **PMDLs** are a selection of scoundrels who bruise egos or even break hearts.

Pre-bound (verb): To find a new job/relationship before ditching the old one.

Pull the ripcord (verb): To decide it is time to exit a gathering. The ripcord may occasionally have to be pulled for you by your **Wingman** if you have been the life and soul of the party a little too long and have suddenly come over all emotional.

Radio Contact: Contact with friends via mobile phone.

Retrosexual: A male who spends the smallest proportion possible of his disposable income on grooming and lifestyle, preferring the caveman approach.

SG: The Single Girl, our heroine.

S&MBF: Straight and Male Best Friend.

Social Hand Grenade: A person who will cause chaos whatever the social setting. Best for an **SG** not to select as a **Wingman**, unless she is mischief making.

Squeaky: A small, stupid female who is a man's woman, rather than a girly girl. Will blank an **SG** if they have a **Distraction** they can flirt with in the vicinity.

Wingman: The person from an **SG**'s friends whom she chooses to accompany her on events/nights out etc. Identity will alter depending on function.

Introduction

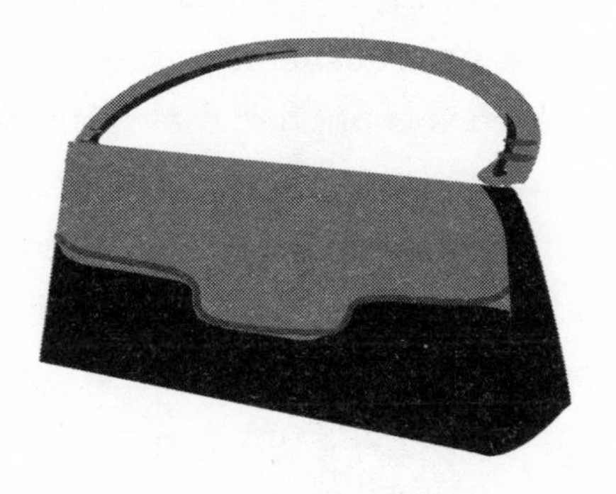

It is a truth which should be universally acknowledged that a single girl can be in possession of the most wonderful life.

The world has moved on from Austen's husband-hunters, and in the last hundred years the **Single Girl (SG)** has begun to garner a more positive status. Thanks to the sexual revolution, her opportunities are becoming endless. No longer does she carry the somewhat derogatory moniker of 'spinster'; we are talking Bridget Jones' singletons and Carrie Bradshaw's sex. Single women are allowing themselves to be celebrated – to a point. Both Bridget and

Carrie only reach fulfilment when they ride off into the sunset with Mr Darcy and Mr Big.

But what if the prince doesn't come or gets a bit delayed? Is the SG to sit and pine? Or waste her time desperately seeking a male specimen in stalker-like fashion, which is enough to make any sensible man sprint in the opposite direction – especially if he hears her biological clock ticking like Peter Pan's crocodile before he even sees her coming? When a relationship is right, it is wondrous. But when it is not, what is the point? You can be lonelier in the wrong relationship than you can ever be when you are single. For when unattached, you can take control, managing your world so as to make the whole universe your oyster, keeping any melancholic black clouds that may have been hovering over your head at bay. Yes, being attached brings its own fun, but as an SG you have so many distinct, delicious possibilities to explore. You may not be unattached forever – so take advantage of the single lifestyle while you can. Seize the day.

I have been single for the best part of the last ten years, almost all my adult life. Yes, I have dated and had relationships in that time, but I have been single the majority of it, and I remain so as I write. I love men – there is nothing so heady and fabulous as being in lust or even love – but I have found it a challenge to encounter worthy ones. I admit, I am fussy, but then again I am fastidious about my handbags, and I would like a male to last longer on my arm than they do. When it comes to boyfriends, you are allowed to be careful.

Being without one is really not the survival test it is made out to be; I could not tell you the last time a friend made me cry, but I could certainly pinpoint when a man did. Moreover, I have witnessed the destructiveness of divorce: choosing to be with someone, maybe making a life with them, is a decision that has to be got right. And if no knight-in-almost-shining-armour comes (no relationship is perfect, but it is important to have a half-decent starting point), I will be OK.

A simple truth. There is, funnily enough, a direct link between the person you breed with and whether the associated offspring turn out to be happy, well-adjusted souls or not. The detractors of women leaving it later to have babies neglect to admit that, half the time, these SGs just did not meet someone who they were confident would be a good father to their offspring. They should be praised for saving society, not screwing it up. And for propping up the shoe industry with their disposable income.

I have not always been of this disposition: the stresses and strains of modern life once overwhelmed this SG. But when everything went wrong I avoided Prozac-popping by, in small steps, managing the parts – and people – of my life that I could, and in time I found myself not just running but sprinting through existence again. This journey has been one hell of a ride and in my decade of research for this book, I have had the most extraordinary experiences and heard (even featured in) the most scandalous tales. Names have been withheld to protect the guilty, but their actions will illustrate how to put sparkle into your SG smile, their anecdotal evidence backing up my practical advice.

This book is not about how to find a man. Tongue embedded firmly in cheek, it is about how to steer a safe passage through the stormy waters of the SG's world, limit the seasickness, and even enjoy the trip. Of course, the side effect of successfully managing your life is that your innate air of confidence will attract at least one male who will want to play to your tune (although they might need a little encouragement/manipulation to get the opening notes right).

The expedition is a comprehensive one. It starts with managing your working life: from handling your boss and obnoxious (especially on Valentine's Day) colleagues to survival skills for that most hideous of inventions, the Work Training Course (WTC), and work functions including the Office Christmas Party, all you need to know to be mistress of the workplace is here.

As SGs, we have the advantage of being able to devote more time to the body beautiful: from medicals to manicures, this is your moment to focus on YOU, and there is a chapter to show you just how to go about it. To attain your inner body beautiful, you will be doing battle with unsympathetic doctors, gynaecologists and a myriad of alternative health gurus. Then there is the creation of the outer body beautiful – from diet and gym etiquette to shopping. When single, you have the benefit of never being made to feel that clothes and shoes are a luxury, or that there are more necessary purchases to be made; instead *they* are a necessity, part of the armour of modern life.

The way you live your life is your call. Home is your domain: if you want, you can take pride in it and perfectly feng shui your pad without fear of a smelly football kit or noisy plastic playthings destroying your ambience. You can go for location and live in a place so small a cat could not reside in it, never mind swing with you in it, or find somewhere that comfortably contains your entire collection of footwear, but which you can neither get a taxi from or to. Whether buying or renting, estate agents need to be played – sorry, managed – so are up for scrutiny. And then to share or not to share... that is the flatmate question.

Family, like everything else, also needs to be managed. This is true whatever one's age or marital status, but especially for a single woman with ovaries still grumbling once a month. Be prepared, in good Girl Guide style, for any curve balls they throw at you and, most importantly, for Festive Season Survival.

Friends, the family you get to pick, are essential – your support network when you are down, your playmates when you want to have fun – but they too need to be managed: found, kept and in some instances dropped. At the very least it is crucial to have certain types of friend: the **Genuine Girlfriends** and perhaps even a **Best Friend (BF)**; a **Gay Best Friend (GBF)** if you can find one;

Platonic Boyfriends and, of course, **Bunbury**. Bunbury, a term coined by Oscar Wilde in *The Importance of Being Earnest*, is an imaginary friend who can provide a convenient excuse or example for almost anything.

From your friends you will choose the right **Wingman** (aka your 'plus one' or your 'Walker') for the right occasion; there is no need to fly solo just because you are single. Being out and having fun is something that we SGs can do better and more often than anyone; we are not beholden to another's diary and body clock. But as such we have standards – we know what a good party is. Thus, remember Bunbury. If choosing whether to attend an occasion, preparation is key, so you must be aware of the dangers of social situations such as going to a restaurant with a ridiculing relative, the Couply Dinner Party, the Hen Night, the Wedding and New Year's Eve; and the measures that can be taken to minimise the damage.

Attending these events will by default put you **in harm's way**, that is, in contact with the male of the species, and it is only natural that you will come across one who is attracted to the happy-in-herself you. There is nothing wrong with having a **Distraction**, an **Object** (of affection), as long as they make you smile. There is a socially acceptable age range for your Distraction (even a mathematical formula) and a melange of advantages and disadvantages to the younger man, the older man, the rich man, the student, the bisexual...

The early stages of a flirtation are on a par with the selection process that the manager of a sporting team embarks upon. A game plan is required to negotiate the peril that is modern-day communication. Used correctly, mobiles and computers can reel in the prey in a marvellous manner, but he-mail banter can be tricky, whilst mobile phones are more akin to unexploded hand grenades.

Dates are littered with potential obstacles, from dinners with chopsticks and garlic noodles to who holds the popcorn at the cinema... And, of course, **kissing** (polite euphemism for anything from kissing to full-blown sex). One messy, complicated, delicious minefield. There is the one-night stand, aka **Accidental Sex (AS)**, the walk of shame, the positively virginal fifth date rule, and then the naughty territory of S&M, sex toys and so on... if you are happy to go that way, fine; escape routes are offered if you are not.

So you are single? At this moment in time, it's all about you. You are not compromising your world for someone who does not appreciate what a catch you are. You have friends who will actually do your DIY for you rather than just look at it; and a Rampant Rabbit that will dependably give you an orgasm, not fall asleep halfway through because of one beer too many (always keep spare batteries). You are whole, not half. You can have the most amazing existence as an SG, firmly guiding yourself away from black clouds and into revelling underneath a bright blue sky. This Single Girl's Guide says hold on tight and be prepared for the ride of your life.

Chapter One

Work Management

The first crucial stepping stone to the SG's conquest of the world – whether debt-ridden graduate or lottery winner – is employment of some description.

Everyone needs a motive to get out of bed, a purpose, a *raison d'être*. It is about feeling valued, not necessarily materially, but mentally. In my early to mid-twenties, I fell apart. Career, health, home and men: all went wrong at once. Black clouds did not just hover over my head; they poured with seemingly endless rain. How did I get out of it? The first move was finding a job, albeit a hideous one, which provided some shield from the storm, gave me time to apply for a better form of employment, allayed some of my family's more vocal concerns, helped me deal with a misdiagnosis courtesy of my doctors – and then everything else began to slot into place.

A job, even if it is not the right one but just a stopgap, makes you feel better about yourself. Packing your day with purpose also prevents you over-analysing your life. Some self-awareness and analysis is a good thing. Too much dwelling, however, can be very bad indeed; life becomes pointless when you ponder on it too long. There is nothing like throwing yourself into work to help take your mind off emotional malaise. A girlfriend of mine who worked for her father got ditched by her long-term boyfriend; her dad wisely tripled her workload. This got her through the shell shock stage, when you have to cope with the very real sense of loss caused by the simple lack of the ex's physical presence. She was soon loving the bachelorette lifestyle. If you are frantically managing the mundane, when you do address weightier issues, it tends to be with a calmer, more balanced perspective – time will have begun to heal the wounds. My friend skipped a large amount of the waterworks phase of her break-up (normally the first few days) because she was just too busy to cry. When she finally found the time to consider the split, she decided, quite rationally, that for her it had been a lucky escape not to be married at 25.

Employment not only satisfies the innate necessity humans have to fill their days; it also brings income and, let us face facts, money is the fuel for your fire. It means you get to remove yourself from the parental home, buy shoes and play. Being with a boyfriend can be wonderful, but there are unique advantages to being without one. A single earning person, in contrast with an attached one, either with or without small people in tow, is afforded blissful privileges. Of course, you still have to part with the chunk of cash that goes to that nasty taxman and mean financial institutions that use the words 'red' and 'debt', and whatever your marital status, everyone has the expense of electricity. However, what remains is all for you. There is no need to justify to a protesting partner the purchase of an accessory rather than an ironing board, or a manicure instead of some new paint. You are not contributing towards football season tickets (unless they are for you).

With no children on the scene, you are neither guilt-ridden in work nor driven insane by baby talk at home, and all disposable income is not channelled into disposable nappies. Jimmy Choo shoes are liable to become firmly unrealisable purchases the minute the patter of tiny feet loom on the horizon. Baby booties will always have to come before leopard print Louboutins.

There may well be an era, namely the rest of your life, when you can berate yourself for not lavishing appropriate time or cash on your partner or children or both, when all you want to do is nurture things that you have bred. Women tend to excel at guilt, so celebrate your moment now. Take pleasure from the knowledge that you are probably never going to feel less at fault, look more glamorous or have the possibility to play more than at this stage of your life.

Finding a Job

Every job, even if it is more like a vocation, has dull bits. If yours is exceptionally boring, then you should view it merely as the launch pad to getting a better one. In the meantime, you must hang on in there. Unlike in relationships, where it is always best to leave if you are at an unhappy dead end, perseverance pays off with jobs. While finding a new boyfriend when still with the old is never clever, and has even less chance of success than a rebound relationship, it is perfectly acceptable and even advisable to take such an approach in the workplace. It is easier to find a new job, to **pre-bound** into a better one, when you are employed elsewhere.

When deciding what you want to do, sound out your most honest friends for a reality check. Even if your particular brand of freak value could make you a *Big Brother* winner, it is no guarantee of any sort of career longevity – just ask Craig of BB1 (who? Exactly). Reach for the stars, but ones which you have a realistic chance of attaining – if you really can sing then pull out the stops to do so before Simon Cowell, just make sure you have a backup plan with more weight than a Rachel Zoe client.

Once you have decided on the path you are taking, be relentless in your pursuit and do not let rejection get you down – in the quest for the perfect job it is just par for the course. Other people will undoubtedly have had the same idea about getting their feet in this particular worthwhile door, so prepare yourself for your toes to be treaded on during the process. Before I finally got my first dream job developing scripts for a film company, I spent years sending out a million CVs never to receive a rejection letter. However, it was not because my phenomenal talents and supreme suitability for the positions were being recognised – the companies concerned were so oversubscribed they just could not be bothered to write back. The worst a potential employer can do is not acknowledge you, next is that they say a slow 'no'. Persist and eventually someone will give you an interview, and in the end, a contract.

Also, remember to enjoy the ride. Life is about the journey; treating it as a competition will only end in tears. Think of success not in terms of what other people think about you, but how you perceive yourself, and if you have tried your hardest and Lady Luck just would not go your way, then forgive yourself. At least you were brave enough to give it a go; no regrets, as Robbie wrote when he departed from Take That. Contend, rather than regret never being a contender. At this point in time you can relish the freedom of only having yourself to consider and are therefore able to take up all the more opportunities. You are not held hostage by what someone else requires of you – so go ahead, do not be afraid to strive for your dream. Since you are single, doors are open to you that may be firmly closed later, such as working abroad for a period. One SG 29-year-old friend of mine recently went off to work for a Prada-wearing devil of a fashionista in New York, something she would never have contemplated doing had she still been with her conventional ex-boyfriend. Not only would he have objected to the serial cocktail party demands on her time – he thought her place was making, not eating, canapés to the extent he even sent her on a cooking course – he got uneasy outside a two mile radius of Chelski football club. She headed for handbags and gladrags and left him to his Russian idols.

Applying for a job can be a job in itself. You can buy books on recruitment but be warned – my GBF was hired to write such tomes when just out of university, never having held or indeed applied for a full-time job.

The application process is basically common sense, however. The short and succinct covering letter helps, as does the relevant CV. A little embellishment really does go a long way. No one is actually going to check if you were president instead of secretary of your school's Literary Society. However, they might just look into your PA job for Colleen 'Rooney'. For backup, bribery of your personal referees is perfectly acceptable; one male friend offered his referee sexual favours, although I would suggest a simple alcoholic beverage is quite sufficient.

On your employment search there is no substitute for networking, which remains key throughout any career. Anyone can network, but you have a massive advantage – being single, you do not have to deal with mate maintenance, and can devote appropriate attention to expanding your address book. I attend on average four evening events a week that will help me workwise. This may seem a lot but then again I work in 'fluffy' industries (by fluffy I refer to the walking cliché that is the 'meeja' world and its members) where many involved don't do daylight hours. Actors and musicians are as nocturnal as vampires; they prefer to perform at night since they then have half a chance of a captive audience and of manipulating the light to maintain their forever-youthful reputations. If you know you have the skills and all you need is the break, then networking will in time come through for you. One A-list theatre director SG I know cultivated contacts left, right and centre stage and eventually got her chance when one revealed that they were resigning from a position that would suit her, my director friend. They stood at a postbox and sent their respective resignation and application letters together. The boss could not believe his luck when both letters appeared and he did not have to go through the hassle of recruiting anyone. The rest is award-laden history.

The Interview

A wise acquaintance once said that interviews are about arriving at a mutually compatible set of lies – which is a first date if ever I heard of one. Since you will have invariably been sharpening your own such skills on the singles scene, you are at an advantage here.

First of all, there is the painstaking attention to your appearance. It is obviously judicious to dress in an outfit you can kick ass in, but appropriately: do not wear a short skirt and stilettos if they will distract you from impressing the interviewer (and them from paying enough attention to your sharp comments rather than your shapely calves). One SG I know has the same uniform for a date as for an interview: trousers, high-heeled boots and adjustable cleavage – the number of buttons done up depending on which tactics she has decided on for either encounter. Think about what they are looking for and dress to fit their ideal; your pinstripe-tastic outfit for a potential job in a bank is not going to be the same as for one at a fashion magazine, where you will sweat or shiver in next season's must-have item (fashionistas work six months ahead, so their clothes cause inappropriate body temperatures). On arrival, make sure your handshake is neither limp nor ball-breaking, which are off-putting in any social setting, but instead firm. Also, maintain good eye contact – who wants someone in their world, working or otherwise, whose eyes are fixed to their feet, even if they are wearing very good shoes?

Then there are the searching questions about your views and actions past and present, to which you respond hopefully eloquently, portraying yourself in the best possible light. A friend of mine who works in human resources typically asks the following: 'What is the most difficult decision you have ever had to make?' The standard response is along the lines of 'Taking a gap year without parental support'. However, one female candidate replied, 'Deciding to go ahead with an abortion.' Not perhaps the best subject matter for an interview (or indeed, first date). It was the only time my HR friend has ever been stunned into silence by an interviewee, who did not get the job – the only reason being that so much of life, especially your working one, demands the ability to self-censor when required. You need to answer in a manner that will show off your suitability for the job, so always try to tie in replies to work-related matters.

Read the trade publications for the industry you are hoping to join and drop in some jargon. One SG friend went through twelve rounds of interviews with an American bank armed merely with a few relevant terms and the gift of the gab. I still doubt that she knows her bulls from her bears, but she remains in their employ because she can sell a pension plan to anyone. Some firms care less about knowledge, and the interview process is more about testing your survival skills. They will thus pride themselves on the number of pointless interviews they will put you through and the level of offensive questions they will ask. During one session at such a firm, a confidant of mine was asked to estimate how many gravediggers were currently working in the UK – she later found out her unfazed guess was the reason she was offered the job.

If you make minor errors, do not let them put you out of your stride – as on dates, they can be endearing. One SG pal was in a job interview and nervously kept banging her foot against the table leg. She thought it was going well as one of the guys interviewing her kept smiling; it was only at the end of the interview that she realised it was actually *his* leg, not the table's, that she had been knocking against. She got the job. As did my fashion PR SG friend who said 'blow job' instead of 'blow-dry' to a particularly attractive male interviewer.

Your interviewer wants to see some personality, so do not be afraid of letting it shine through. Imagine you are the twentieth in a long line of interviewees and are asked by the rather bored head of HR, 'What is your greatest achievement?' Rather than saying 'Running the marathon', think of something a little more entertaining, like talking your way into the VIP section at Glastonbury and having Orlando Bloom admire your wellington boots. You can then bring it back to work, saying that it displays your tenacity, but it also shows you have spark. These people are going to have to spend at least nine hours a day with you, so would undoubtedly prefer an interesting, lively addition to the team to someone dull with a touch of the sanctimonious about them.

Lastly, it will not hurt in the least that you are single – in an HR manager's eyes you might be seen as more likely to preoccupy yourself with work instead of being immersed in wedding planning hell or the worry that you are missing little Leo's first step.

Well done, you have managed to land The Job. Now you have to manage your working life. Work/life balance can be tricky to achieve, but thankfully there are short cuts.

Boss Management

Bosses are no different to parents, friends and other people in your world – they all need to be managed. Some may call this manipulation, but that implies cruelty. There is nothing cruel about making sure that your world is running in a satisfactory manner. When you have the people in your life playing to your tune, you are being effective, which is what a boss wants.

There tends to be two types of boss – easy and tricky. The former are usually male, the latter female.

Male bosses are a bizarre mix of fathers and boyfriends, usually displaying typical traits of each. They can thus be wound round your little finger, but at the same time are prone to occasional bouts of unreasonable behaviour. However, they are far less likely than the female of the species to hold a grudge long term and this makes managing them much simpler.

They are often concerned primarily with style; how things are perceived. Minutiae are normally not their game – they want the big picture right first and foremost, and as long as the small stuff is executed, are less likely to sweat about how you go about it. Most can be easily managed with friendly banter, brutal efficiency and occasional flattery/flirting. (Flirting does not mean sleeping with, which is almost always a very bad plan indeed. If you are having an affair with your boss, please refer to Chapter Eight.)

If you need something done, or a decision from a male boss, often making them feel it is their idea is the way forward. Bosses are human; like everyone else they like to feel valued. Be lavish in praise to your boss, always emphasising their importance to your good work, how you benefit from their mentoring... even if this is not wholly true. They will then magnanimously give you some credit where it is due. Become the mistress of the art of suggestion, planting the idea in their heads that you need funding for a new project/overtime/promotion, so they either think the brainwave is all theirs and suggest it themselves, or are more amenable when you approach them about it. Accomplish this by e-mailing them a few early morning or evening messages, thus demonstrating your commitment, discussing with them how you feel you can improve, and subtly pointing out how well you compare to those just above you in the work pecking order. They should be putty in your hands.

Some men are old school in outlook, and have preconceived notions about women and their roles in the workplace. When a male boss's behaviour becomes particularly objectionable, it can be a struggle to suppress the urge to drill a stiletto heel into his head with frustration. SGs can confuse them, with certain bosses even entertaining the notion that you are merely killing time whilst husband-hunting. But before you lift that stilettoed foot, stop. You can often turn these attitudes around to your advantage. You do not have to break down barriers; you are brighter than that – you will figure out how to walk around them.

For instance, men, specifically older ones, claim they are no good at typing when they are actually perfectly proficient. I was once a useless secretary, and my boss would dictate to me his e-mails as he claimed he was a slow one-fingered typer. This was a lie; I know for a fact that he was actually quite speedy, being caught out using as many as eight fingers at once on occasion.

I was initially irritated, and then I realised I could profit from this. I was copied in on all high-level, confidential e-mails and learnt a huge amount that came into seriously good use on subsequent job-hunting, when it was clear that my knowledge could be a real asset to any potential employer. Of course, whilst I was still at the company, the information I was privy to meant that I was a proper power player. I may have had to make cups of tea for my boss, but I never had to make my own. The rest of the office pandered to my every hot drink need, and I often found copious quantities of chocolate on my desk; I knew of every major decision before everyone else and making an ally of me could be very useful. Whatever your boss's flaws, find a way to use them to your advantage.

If the male boss is about style, the female boss is about substance; they care about the minutiae *and* the big picture. That does not mean that they cannot be managed, just that it is harder, and unless you do it well, they will probably spot what you are up to a mile off; to get where they are, they will have played all the same games. Usually the female boss will be a cross between a particularly ugly sister and, if you are really unlucky, a stepmonster with a grudge. Their attention to detail is likely to be far more acute than a male boss's and it is essential to keep them on your side. Cover your back – if it is a challenging work environment where they need to be ruthless to survive, make sure that they cannot make you the sacrificial cow. Thus be meticulous in your dealings so that mistakes that are not yours can never be attributed to you, conscientious in keeping the female boss in the loop – they like to know what is going on because they are thinking about everything that is going on – and deferent. Do not raise their hackles and antagonise their natural female competitive instinct by dressing in your most drop dead gorgeous attire – keep it professional, otherwise it could be the kiss of career death. Ostensibly at least, never have a better handbag nor more functional love life, and under no circumstances ever flirt with their other halves. However, although they might be the harder taskmistresses, when you really need it – especially if it will enhance their reputation – they may well support you to the hilt. And you could have the female boss who is one of the occasional exceptions to the rule – I once had a truly lovely one, who years later still takes me out to dinner.

Colleague Management

Common sense dictates that it is essential to keep anyone who works with you, directly or indirectly, on your side. Not only does this make for a more pleasant working environment, but in the case of those who work under you, it also means they are more likely to accept the tasks you delegate to them; thus allowing you to e-mail and phone your friends – erm, I mean leave the office on time – and attain that elusive work/life balance. They will also save your bacon, by going to fetch you some in a butty and covering your incompetence if you are battling the hangover from hell.

Appearances are everything. Managing your working world means being perceived to be working at an effective but maximum capacity. Being overworked does no one nor any business any good, especially if you are in a job you do not like. You are single and do not want to be too exhausted to revel in your status after hours.

There are a number of tactics to make sure everyone knows you have reached maximum capacity without resorting to whinging, which will just antagonise everyone in your vicinity. If you have a phone on which you can send and receive e-mail, make sure you fix the settings so that it will be clear to the recipient when you have sent a message from the device. For instance, every e-mail from a Blackberry phone ends with the words 'Sent from my Blackberry® wireless device'. You should then send such missives at slightly obscure hours, as it will make you look extremely busy but nonetheless on top of things. If you get in to work early or stay late, make sure you e-mail key people as soon as you arrive or just before you depart so they realise the hours you are putting in. And, if you are getting overloaded in the office, send holding e-mails saying that you cannot resolve the query now, but it is on your mind. Wherever you go during working hours, make sure you are holding a piece of official looking paper and wearing a purposeful expression. It will dawn on colleagues that you are swamped, but that you are doing your best to do good business and to maintain good contact. They are then far more likely to come to your rescue than if you had stropped.

Appreciate your colleagues. It is the post room person, the IT guys and the work experience boys and girls who make the working world go round. Make sure they are invited to team lunches and drinks, and remember birthdays. Whether it be the tea boy or PA, look after them – not only yours, but other people's. One associate of mine was brokering a deal with a particularly irritating attorney in New York; she made friends with his executive assistant after discovering they both had a Daniel-Craig-dressed-in-trunks fetish. After clogging up their companies' e-mail systems sharing photos of the new James Bond, she found her calls were always returned and the deal was done. One of my SG friend's PA is essential to my well-being, even getting me tables in fully-booked restaurants when only corporate pulling power will sway the maître d'. My SG friend rarely gets a Christmas card from me, but I always send her PA one.

It is the smallest kindness that can foster the biggest amount of good will, and food is the cheapest and easiest smile maker. If you occasionally bring back sweets from the newsagent, or biscuit tubs from M&S for everyone to share, people will put themselves out that much more for you. When I organise a theatre workshop, where everyone is giving his or her time for free, I always make sure the food is plentiful and delicious. An actor's performance will inevitably scale shiny statuette-worthy heights thanks to Percy Pig sweets.

Everyone exploits their own repertoire of skills, and in your efforts to get others in your workplace dancing to your tune, remember yours. You are single, and some friendly flirtation is not going to hurt anyone. I am not suggesting you cross professional lines, but people do business with people who attract them in some way – financially and, indeed, personally. A stunning SG friend of mind who sacrificed supermodelling for stockbroking is regularly the only woman in meetings. She wears the smartest suits, the sharpest stilettos, and normally gets her way by cajoling. Sometimes, of course, flirting will not get the required response, and these men will play the macho card and try to impose their way, at which point she is prepared to dig those heels in. She always arrives armed with a game plan, only concedes as much as she planned to before the meeting began and finds the room typically acquiesces to her demands. If it does not, it needs to know my friend will walk away rather than be walked over. If she has to resort to this tactic, she almost always gets a phone call within hours agreeing to her proposal.

Work is not a place to display chinks in your armour, but some colleagues will try to find them, no matter how many chocolate chip cookies you hand out. However wound up you get, never let them see you cry, even if you are shouted at; that is what bathroom breaks are for. Since you are single, some colleagues will decide that this is the topic they can tease you on. Your refusal to settle in the wrong relationship shows strength of character, but many people who have not exercised such good sense are threatened by this, and will try to use it against you. One SG hairdresser friend had a male manager who gave her a really hard time about her status and any supposed after hours naughtiness she may have got up to, while a fellow male stylist with a predilection for the GCSE work experience girls was always applauded for his extra-curricular activities. Most of the time the SG simply bantered back, but if she ever needed to shed a tear she would retreat to the ladies, or as was more usually the case, leave the premises on a chocolate run so she could emit a scream of frustration. Obvious signs of distress only ever made them heckle her all the more.

The office does not get more obnoxious than on Valentine's Day, when work colleagues (especially those who have just added a piece of jewellery to the third finger of their left hand) become unbearable. With the good manners that they have failed to extend to you by flagrantly flaunting their attached status, cordially congratulate them, whilst quietly remembering that any occasion demanding jollity as a prerequisite rarely is jolly – even if it involves presents (25 December) or sex (14 February). The SG holds the upper hand on Valentine's Day; no expectation means no disappointment – pity the girl across the office whose long-term boyfriend delivers nothing more than some dead flowers from the local garage. If you want to fight back by showing off something tangible from someone who loves you, employ the reciprocal arrangement whereby you and a friend send each other a delivery of flowers/chocolates/gift of your choosing to the office, and when it arrives you can be as mysterious as you like. Attached people will get jealous – remember, being single means that everything is possible. You may still end up with Christian Slater; they cannot, as they have settled for Wayne from IT.

As well as the loved-up colleagues, you may be sharing the office with the proud parent kind, who will ceaselessly bang on about their little ones. They have to remind you regularly about their offspring as they are justification for: being late for work; looking a mess; taking time off over half-term and Christmas. Remain silent, coo over the pictures when you need something from them, and get holiday requests in early. If these parents are really getting to you, go out during lunch, buy a new pair of shoes, and proceed to show them off to everyone round the office when you get back, leaving them to look forlornly at their lunchtime purchase – nappies from Boots.

The Work Training Course

The WTC can be the bane of the single person's life. As there are no needy people at home requiring your prompt presence both morning and night, you will be earmarked as a particularly suitable person to attend these typically pointless affairs.

There is a peculiar rule, when it comes to WTCs. The more serious and 'worthy' the industry – banking, accountancy, law – the more ridiculous the training courses its employees are subjected to. The more frivolous the business – television, PR, theatre, music – the more relevant, indeed seriously useful, they will be.

There are extraordinary tales about WTCs from those in 'proper' jobs. An SG banker I know was taught circus skills, including juggling, whilst another had to do things with Lego. As a lawyer friend of mine says, 'You know you are in trouble when they ask you to bring warm, waterproof clothing and a torch.' How is climbing Snowdonia and hospitalising yourself with hypothermia going to make you a better financier? One SG friend who works in commercial property was sent dragon boat racing, where teams have to get into small boats and row to the rhythm of a drum. All the men in the lone SG's group got so competitive and thought their abilities so superior, they insisted that she stand on the riverbank while they took part. The SG complained enough to make her point that this was not very 'team-building' in spirit, but not so much that she would actually have to physically partake in the exercise in any way and left them to it. The men they packed the boat with were so heavy it sank, whilst the landlubber cried with laughter and, on top of getting a soaking, these testosterone-overloaded souls got a dressing down by those in charge for not including the SG.

Thus if you work for a 'serious' profession, and are told to go on a WTC, do everything you can to get out of it. You will learn nothing that a day off watching *Richard & Judy* could not teach you.

There are two reliable paths the SG can take to absent herself. The first is to play the martyr; get a hamstring injury and offer to go, but emphasise that you will not be able to participate in any of the physical activities and will need to remain in the hotel watching daytime television. Otherwise, when presented with the date, *immediately* respond that there is a wedding/funeral/family thing that you have no choice but to attend. One solicitor **Girl Playmate** of mine with a notoriously messed up family always gets out of her WTCs by saying she has to attend family therapy; with her relatives it is utterly believable.

Nevertheless, at some stage during your career – whatever the industry – you will probably have to go on the occasional WTC in order to keep your job. At least hope it is not an overnighter, or if it is, that it is somewhere good like Cannes.

If you are fortunate, you will get regular breaks so you can check your Blackberry and get some work done, as well as munch on good biscuits. If there are no biscuits, seriously consider staging a protest – the whole point of a WTC is the biscuits.

The person who runs the WTC will be a **Joiner**, and they pose a unique challenge to the SG. Joiners are team players who relish outdoor group activities whatever the weather, and are advocates of 'enforced fun'. Enforced fun is not a term I have made up. I first heard it from a (married) someone who runs the WTCs for a massive management consultancy firm, one of those that are extremely good at haemorrhaging tax payers' money on governmental reports. As an SG, you have an innate sense of what fun is as you have the time to go out and have quite a lot of it, and you understand that it cannot be enforced – how many people actually enjoy New Year's Eve? Fun is organic, spontaneous – it cannot be planned. Thus a clash of personalities is inevitable at WTCs, and you will wish to rebel against the person in charge.

It is only natural to regress to your school-days' self on a WTC, but try not to become the naughty person at the back of the class, however tempting it may be. You do need to keep your job and putting any perfectly behaved co-workers' backs up will not be helpful in the long run. Equally, avoid turning into a teacher's pet; no one likes Little Miss Smug, including the 'teacher'. I know of one person in charge who almost came to blows with a particularly bright spark who infuriated him beyond reason during a WTC; he could not make a statement without a hand springing up or an unhelpful interjection being made. However, instead of a black eye, the attendee had a far more bitter pill to swallow – his funding was cut on the instructor's recommendation. Occasionally make a pertinent point, attempt willingness at allocated tasks, but if they are getting too ridiculous plead that real work beckons and take the opportunity to go and make loud calls to the office.

Work Events

Although there is a chapter specifically on Event Management, work events are so entwined with work politics as a whole that the examination of them has to go here. As briefly touched upon, the dream job, deal or project is liable in some way to result from networking. If you are seen at the right events, talk to the right people and make the right contacts, it will eventually pay off – and you could even find yourself having fun along the way. Contacts can come from the most obscure places. While working on a theatre project, I found the perfect director when I trod on his toe at midnight at a party. The project in question had come about after I met the writer's agent in a gay nightclub in Marrakech on New Year's Eve whilst dancing to Madonna's 'Hung Up'. If I had spent both nights in under my duvet, as had been tempting, my career – and indeed life

– would have turned out very differently indeed.

Admittedly these examples are somewhat unusual, but whatever your industry, there will be social events. It is essential for your own benefit to go to at least a few official 'work drinks', but you certainly do not need to attend all, and as with WTCs, a little forethought will ensure your absence if necessary.

Betrothed and babied-up colleagues have their own standard covers for excusing themselves from work events, but SGs also have certain tricks at their disposal. If the gathering in question is a somewhat official occasion, and is not only going to be dire but will also fail to help you climb the career ladder in any way, say that you cannot make it because you are 'at the theatre/opera'. Never the cinema or on a date, both of which in many people's minds are cancellable activities. The theatre or opera, however, implies that you are scholarly and cultured and you are far less likely to be challenged when you change for the outing in the loos at work and totter back through the office catwalk in all your finery. Never mind that you retire at the interval to the nearest pub as it is an appalling production starring an American sitcom star who has never stood on a stage in his life; snobbery is alive and well and people will accept your absenteeism.

For the more useful social events on the work calendar, your presence does not have to be negotiated with a stroppy other half or snivelling child; your evenings are your own and if you want to attend, you can. Furthermore, on the occasions you do choose to grace a work event with your presence, everyone will be suitably grateful as you can be relied on to 'give good value'. I will explain.

SGs can make the time to always shine. Unlike more personal-responsibility-overloaded colleagues, before you arrive at the affair, you will be able to do some extra homework. Research who is going, why and what they want from it. Work out what you yourself need to gain from the gathering and with all this in mind compile a **Conversation List** (**CL**). This should include a number of questions for you to ask, and a list of replies to enquiries that might be aimed in your direction. This list does not have to be something you write down – it can simply be a thought process – but it is an invaluable tool in many areas of life; a steering mechanism to keep discussions on a track you are comfortable with. Your prior preparation means that there are never any embarrassing pauses in conversation – unless it serves your purposes – and it is easier to procure any pertinent information that you may need from the rendezvous. It prevents you from panicking, inadvertently becoming overly aggressive and filling in awkward silences with unsuitable utterances. A little cool, calculated conversation management is all that is required to achieve your desired outcome from the gathering.

It is rare for SGs to find our sex and sexuality – our (relatively) youthful good looks and single status – does not become a factor at all with evening events; indeed they can make them a veritable minefield. We deal with crossing the 'work–colleague line' when we discuss the male of the species in later chapters, but with some forward planning, including a CL, a safe path can usually be negotiated through work events, whether ties or trainers (or both if you work in advertising) are compulsory.

At the glamour end of the spectrum, the supermodel stockbroker is regularly invited by a lawyer associate to accompany him to the opera, where his firm has sponsored seats. She suspects he is infatuated, but thanks to her groundwork – the CL, the high-necked and ankle-skimming outfits, and the escape strategy (a pre-ordered little black bus) – the possibility of him making inappropriate advances are averted. At meals with her office colleagues, she always leaves immediately after the dinner, before all the men on her team decide to go to a strip joint. This sort of situation is something we all have to deal with to some degree, whether it means fending off someone on an overnight WTC or leaving the lads you work with in the pub to get seriously lashed once you have had a swift after-work sharpener with them. You are free – to stay out with them or go home and curl up with a tub of Ben & Jerry's and *Point Break* if you so desire. All useful networking will have taken place before you leave anyway – men tend to get memory loss by the third pint, and if they are off to a location as salubrious as Stringfellows, are probably already in the forgetful zone.

If you are a single female, the business lunch or dinner provides another test – especially if you are the only woman there. Your companions may be less sure about how to pitch their behaviour if confronted with a together, gorgeous SG in such an intimate social setting, so you need to take control and make sure they cross no inappropriate boundaries. It is all too easy to make the wrong impression. At the end of one meal a particularly bubbly SG friend's boss asked her up to his hotel room to 'drink the mini-bar dry' – he had mistaken her friendliness for a come-on. Unlike in an interview, which has all the hallmarks of a date, if you are at a work meal keep in mind that your behaviour must be the opposite to that of potential lover. Coyly deliberating with your companion about what you want to eat will make you look indecisive; if you tend to get in a flux every time you see a menu try looking up the restaurant's offerings on the Internet first so you can choose beforehand. It is vital for appearances' sake to order your easy-to-eat courses (you do not want to be slathering spaghetti over your chin) within seconds, close your menu, and quickly steer discussions into work areas. Note here that if you eat red meat, a rare steak will do wonders for your killer instinct reputation – one SG I know was headhunted because she ordered hers bloody. Do not have pudding unless the rest of the table decide to first, as you will otherwise risk being seen as a time waster. Try to stay sober, or at least interchange wine with water; work events are just that, work, and they need to be orchestrated. Getting drunk and wrapping a loose tongue around a date is one thing; having a loose tongue at a work event is something else entirely.

If partners are invited to the event, be careful when dealing with your colleagues' and with choosing whom you bring as your 'plus one'. Do not invite either a professional escort or a **Social Hand Grenade** to your party. The former you will always be found out on, and the latter will inevitably create difficulties if you abandon them even for an instant. One SG friend left her mischievous platonic male 'plus one' whilst she went to powder her nose; when she returned everyone at the table was looking at her oddly. She later discovered he had told them that she had always fancied him and that, apart from a one-night stand when they had done it doggy style, she really wasn't his type. The girl left the company soon after.

It is probably best, after initial pleasantries have been exchanged, to politely ignore your female work colleagues' partners; you do not want any light banter to be misconstrued by the women you work with as flirting. When it comes to your male colleagues' other halves, you must ensure that these women know that you are not a threat and you are not going to have an affair with their husband/boyfriend in the workplace. You are a glamorous SG, and that will naturally disturb them – you will be spending more hours with their partners than they do. They will think you fancy their husbands even when for you it would be a physical impossibility; remember, they find them attractive in some way, even if you could never, so tread carefully around them. They perceive you as a predator, and thus you have no margin of error in your dealings with one. Never ask what she does or when the baby is due, unless you are absolutely sure that she does have a job or that she is pregnant. One of my friends, a fresh-faced recruit recently out of university, was at a work drinks party where the wine was flowing and some exceedingly good honey and mustard sausage canapés were doing the rounds. Then, a schoolgirl error; she asked the boss's wife, 'When is it due?' The older woman was momentarily confused and then replied, 'Oh, I am not pregnant! I'm just fat.' Fresh-faced recruit eventually left the organisation – for some strange reason promotion was never forthcoming. If the person inquiring had been carrying post-baby weight or partner-padding too (matching a boyfriend's eating habits plays havoc on the waistline), they would probably have got away with the faux pas.

Occasionally it will be impossible to convince these women you are not after their man, as some married and attached girls are just very unstable. There is an extreme, but nevertheless true, example of a journalist confidant of mine who got fired because the wife of her particularly ugly boss decided she was having an affair with him. This was absolutely ridiculous – he looked like an old, fat frog, and my journalist friend, the top totty of Fleet Street, was madly in lust with a smooth-bodied Adonis. The boss's wife began calling journo-girl up at all hours, even while she was in bed with the Greek god, and then threatened to hit her when she bumped into them at a work function.

Event survived, remember the manners-maketh-man mantra your mother drummed into you when you were small as she instructed you to write thank you letters to obscure relatives for dull toys at Christmas. Always e-mail, or better yet write a real-life thank you note as soon as possible to whomever organised the event. Also, drop a line to people whose business cards you have collected. Occasionally it pays to organise get-togethers yourself, although it is an error to be the one who always does it; you do not want to land yourself with unnecessary responsibility. People should be pleased if you arrange something, aware that your single status means you will always have something – or someone – better to do.

Despite all these guidelines, it is, of course, possible to mess up, and there is one place that is more of a minefield than most.

The Office Christmas Party

This gets a subsection all to itself, although if there are any international editions of this book it will be edited out. The ramifications of this almost always hideous event have a special resonance in the UK; elsewhere, such as in the US, people are usually too afraid to do anything embarrassing or riskworthy for fear of making a bad impression in front of the boss during the annual ritual. It's a shame that back in Blighty we do not posses such self-preservational skills.

If you can get through the Christmas period without being permanently pissed, then you have nerves of steel. For all parties, but especially the office one, I suggest sticking to champagne (if by some miracle the boss splashes out); hopefully the booze budget will be Scrooge-like enough to swiftly run out and you will not have to drink any more. Plus there will come a point when everyone else is so drunk they will not notice that you have moved on to the sparkling water with ice and lemon.

In the UK, the most badly behaved person is usually the boss and the stories of their horrific festive behaviour are innumerable. A secretary I know always has to order her boss a 'vomit cab' – some firms, for a vast puke premium, will supply them during the merry season for passengers they would normally refuse owing to their indecent level of inebriation.

How you use your single freedom during this period is up to you – you have the option of taking the seasonal spirit that much further than the attached, and are allowed to indulge in physical encounters with the opposite sex. However, it helps if he is single too and if you would be happy to lunge at him in any other month. If he would make your blood run cold in January, a mistletoe moment in December is not going to warm the heart for any longer than it takes for the hangover to kick in.

Accidents will happen at this time of year. Keep your mobile handy to take pictures of any scandalous behaviour from your workmates, as you may need to bribe someone not to shout about your own, plan your exit strategy, and just get out as soon as possible. It is all over for another year and you can spend the coming months getting your body beautiful back in shape.

Chapter Two

Mind Over Matter Management

We SGs have the advantage of being able to devote a plentiful proportion of our time to the body beautiful – to our physical and mental health, to our grooming, to our very being.

When you're an SG, you can concentrate wholeheartedly on sorting YOU out from top to toe, both internally and externally. We have enough energy to ensure we are in peak condition and are time-rich enough to address the essential, from making sure we do make that appointment for that ailment to the less necessary, but nevertheless important, anti-ageing treatment that a manic mum or stressed spouse may be forced to neglect. We do not have to sport them, but painted nails and a pair of sharp stilettos do wonders for our sense of self worth; if we look fabulous, we feel fabulous, we are fabulous.

For the time being we are not sharing our bathrooms with large, smelly Neanderthals from whom we have to hide thrush and hair removing cream, or with small children who disgorge mess from every orifice. Furthermore, we have the money to buy products with pretty packaging and organic health food that makes us feel virtuous despite an overindulgence in vodka the night before.

With the money saved from avoiding the pram and PlayStation payment plans, you can treat yourself. Take up a new trivial (or positively practical) pursuit – learn to fly or salsa, or just get a course of massages. It is up to you; you can lavish attention on yourself. This is your moment to indulge; there is no need to suppress the selfish gene. You will never be as young as you are or look as good as you do right now, so enjoy it. Yes, it is important to be realistic – we are never going to look like one of the airbrushed creatures in magazines (OK, I have done in one photo – see book cover) – but in truth, as I can absolutely attest, they have been digitally altered to the extent that the models can barely recognise themselves in these pictures. It is all about managing what you have got, to give you the confidence to live your life the way you want to. And, as Uma Thurman's Swedish goddess of a character in *The Producers* sings, when you've got it... flaunt it.

Mortal Management

Your physical and mental health are the most vital things you will ever manage and are inextricably linked: a happy state of mind tends to promote good health. Not only are both these qualities essential to your maximum enjoyment of SG status now, they will also ward off problems later in life. As the SG quite rightly flourishes into her thirties and beyond, she may wish to reserve the right to breed another being at a subsequent stage. It is absolutely laudable to wait until the conditions are conducive in your world for producing happy offspring, ensuring you have the right mindset and partner – however, this makes it vital that you look after your body now. One girlfriend of mine gave herself a thirty-fifth birthday present of having some of her eggs frozen. With her track record of boyfriends, it is sensible – inflicting an innocent child with any of the paternal candidates she has dallianced with so far would be downright cruel.

You are the person who cares most about you, who knows better than anyone how your body feels, thus the onus is on you to get to grips with any problems that you might have. Doctors do not know everything; this became apparent when I met people trying to become them at university. Every medical student of my generation at Cambridge seemed to 'bin' the leg lectures, as it was the last topic taught on the course. If you ever have a leg problem and it is a Cambridge medic of the late twentieth century sitting on the other side of the desk from you, do not let them near your limb. Seeing my contemporaries become doctors made me realise they are human – and fallible – and it began to dawn on me it may be wise to manage the medical 'profession'.

If you are sick, being single is an additional strain; there is no one with whom you can automatically share your strife. Do not forget you have friends and family who will be there to help – so if you feel the need, ask for it. You would do the same for them. However, sometimes, if you are trying to establish a prognosis, you may not want to worry anyone, and at this point, there are some SG tactics to employ.

The most crucial CLs the SG will ever create are those she composes for doctors. My GP's surgery is right opposite my old school, and every time I go in to see him my legs turn to jelly and I feel like a talentless teenager again. (That school seems to leave similar scars on all its ex-pupils, or my friends at least – one craves cider whenever she walks past it, whilst another will take a detour rather than risk a run-in with the fearsome French mistress.) From bitter experience of never asking the right question, and always being in a nervous state,

I now write down and take in a list of queries, and then diligently take notes from his answers. To help me compose an effective CL, I glean some of my information from the web (although it is vital you do not always believe what you read), some from my friends. If it has got to the stage of a problem where you think you will not be able to take in anything a doctor says – what to do about the lump I found in my breast being my prime example – it is time to bring a confidant to do the asking and listening at the appointment for you. And please note, however tempting it may be, self-medicating is never clever – one SG I know decided to actually answer a spam e-mail and buy Viagra online, having read that combined with a vibrator it would generate an orgasm unlike any other she had ever experienced. It was: the experience was more organ-numbing than earth-moving, although – clouds and silver linings – the junior doctor dealing with her case did have a touch of the Clooneys about him, and when she got over her embarrassment she thoroughly enjoyed (all of) him.

Along with your CL, remember to consider your underwear; I once went for a scan and was wearing a Snoopy G-string. You will find medical experts immune to hairy legs and sprouting bikini lines, but a grinning Snoopy from your crotch area will poleaxe even the most po-faced of professionals.

Probably the worst doctor experience you will come across at this stage of your life is the gynaecologist. Not only can encounters with them be painful but you are an SG, who may well have had sex with more than one partner since her last visit and would rather not regale a stranger with her sexual habits. If the person on the other side of the desk is exuding the air of a Mother Superior, keep in mind it is not their business to give you a morality lesson. As long as you are happy and healthy, which is what you are there to confirm or ensure, it does not matter what they think. Besides, however promiscuous you are, they will have a patient who is much more so than you. And they are probably jealous of the fun you are having.

It is only natural that you may feel somewhat isolated when you want to share serious issues. There is nothing wrong with visiting a therapist; if there was a social stigma attached to having one, it is long gone. There are so many different types – from those with official medical qualifications to lifestyle coaches – and acquiring one is completely acceptable. Indeed, to some they are a veritable accessory. One SG I know goes to a business therapist merely because of the contacts she picks up in the waiting room. She even dated a man she met by the water cooler there, but had to ditch him because he yelled out 'show me the money' at every opportunity, including during sex.

If you can afford to do it, paying someone to listen to you complain has distinct advantages – for instance you can focus more of your time with your friends on playing, and less on bending their ears. Another SG, a stressed out model booker, credits her weekly therapy sessions for how she is generally in control of her world and the starving, snappy people in it. If something upsets her, she decides she will deal with it in that appointed hour, and often when she gets to her appointment she cannot remember why she was so perturbed in the first place, and she and her therapist just have a good gossip. Before she had a shrink, she loathed her tendency to get a bit weepy mid-week; now she has it in check, she feels more in command and happier in general.

The first session with any therapist, when you have to explain to them what has brought you to their door, is always the worst, but from then on it tends to be plainer sailing. If it is not, ditch them. I was told I was anorexic and sent into therapy, when I actually had a thyroid problem (doctors have been known to misdiagnose). I stalked out on the first two therapists as I felt they failed to listen – one was a proponent of a therapy called Cognitive Behavioural Therapy, or CBT, which I dubbed CJD as I thought she treated me like a mad cow. Therapist three thought to question the anorexia – and only then was the real problem discovered and dealt with.

Alternative Therapy

The SG can also be faced with deciding alone whether or not to see alternative practitioners, and if guru types, from masseuses to mediums, might help them. You have only one body, and it is your responsibility and your right to be fussy, so, as with doctors, scrutinise any alternative health practitioner's records carefully, giving most weight to any personal recommendations you may glean. You are then, again, perfectly within your rights to see several to determine whose advice is best for you. Many of these therapists are rapidly becoming the norm – witness Gwyneth Paltrow's 'cupping', a form of alternative pain therapy – but be wary of the guru gurus: those who encompass alternative religions such as scientology, auras, **Horrorscopes** and so forth. They remain less socially acceptable for a reason, and you, the SG, are a prime target since you are without partner and tweenagers to laugh you out of following them. By the same token, be wary that, as an SG, you do not use an 'expert', whether self- or degree-acclaimed, to fill a perceived gap in your world and let them into it to the extent that they dictate to you. You are looking for balance, so you do not have to do everything they say – it took months for myself and my friends to convince an SG, who had been ordered by a 'nutritionist' to only eat raw food, that there is nothing wrong with the odd steak or glass of red wine. It was only when the SG concerned literally turned orange because of the number of carrots she was consuming, that she resumed normal vodka, lime and soda duty. Remember, these people are not there to stress you out because you are unable to follow everything they advise; they are there to enhance your life. The battle for good health is more often than not taking the time to just pause and listen. Not to what everyone else is telling you, but to what your body is, then researching how best you can help it.

Surface Management

You have a beautiful inside; now for the outside. As an SG, you have the time and the cash to be the envy of your married/attached friends who have babies and males eating into their hair-drying and bra-buying time. This is the moment you can get your skin smooth, your clothes becoming and your make-up flawless.

On creating your body beautiful, the GBF comes into his own, so if you can, find one. It may be a stereotype, but it is one friends-of-Dorothy habitually live up to – every Grace can do with a Will, and all Wills love having a Grace to boss about. The GBF will be honest about what you are wearing/how fat you are/your cellulite; it is rare a woman will, for risk of causing offence or receiving a worse retort.

In my experience, often enough it is the GBFs who will have the number, on speed dial, of the best waxer in town – they have thicker hair... and are male, so have a lower pain threshold. Of course, being single, you can go for the painless Italian option in regards to body hair – fabulous on the outside, a gorilla underneath (as the author Kathy Lette says, it's the only time it is ever socially acceptable to proclaim 'bring back Bush'). The Brazilian bikini wax hurts, however many Nurofen Plus you pop, but you do not actually have to do it unless it makes you feel better about yourself. This type of quick fix can extend to other areas, for instance only self-tanning your face and bits on display.

When you enter a beauty salon, do not let a tyrannical therapist alarm you with an insistence that you need more than you have booked, nor that you should purchase a truckload of products from them that you will never use. There is also no need for embarrassment on your part, even if you are ordered onto your hands and knees on their treatment table half naked with your bottom in the air so they can reach some tricky tufts. Rest easy in the knowledge that they will have examined worse ingrown hair, thicker bikini lines and bigger bunioned feet – just make sure your nooks and crannies are clean when you submit yourself to their hands. You are paying and possibly (absolutely in the case of a good waxer) tipping them, so if they make you feel uncomfortable, find a new one. Good bedside manners should extend from physicians to beauticians.

Be slightly wary if your beautician comes from another land, or you are having a treatment abroad – matters can get lost in translation. There is no international language of waxing, so as well as making sure your waxer is properly trained (third-degree burns are not worth a discount, nor the mirth of your latest lover), get specific. A Brazilian wax, which to a European therapist means landing strip remaining, is not the same to a waxer hailing from Hollywood, where the same word means everything off. This particularly agonising experience is termed 'a Hollywood' to girls this side of the pond; I have yet to establish what this term means to someone from California. All I know is that I was left bald in a place I felt should have a little hair when a La-La land therapist got her hands on me at my local London salon.

Along with the treatments themselves, socially acceptable salon behaviour can differ on every continent. Whilst on a business trip to LA I decided to nip to the hotel spa and was confronted with a disclaimer form asking if I used recreational drugs or alcohol and to tick 'yes' or 'no'. In my mind a glass of red wine is completely different to **hoovering** a vast quantity of cocaine, but obviously not to Angelenos. Turn up to a massage in Thailand stark naked as you would in Sweden, and you will find no oil in sight, just a very small and resolute looking woman waving a pair of pyjamas for you to dress in, who proceeds to bend you into positions you never thought possible outside the Kama Sutra. As in everything, it is all about the research, so some may prove prudent before you enter the doors of any salon or spa.

Most of your beauty routine will of course take place in your own bathroom, where you should take the opportunity of being inside such a safety zone to make honest assessments about your look. If your make-up is the same as it was five years ago, you are stuck in a rut, so find a friend who does theirs fabulously to instruct you how to change it. One SG I know had been using the same make-up look she had got from a *Just Seventeen* annual aged 14, until an imperious but well-groomed 23-year-old took her in hand and overhauled her face paint routine. *Just Seventeen* girl was 33. Which just goes to show, what suited you during an era where big shoulder pads and even bigger hair were considered the height of fashion will not necessarily bring out the best in you now.

As an SG, you can makeover to your heart's content, from your heels to your hair, unaffected by a strident spouse. You can hit the hairdresser's and get a style that suits you, with no fear of upsetting a boy who prefers blonde to brunette or who finds passion-killing hilarity in the fact that your collars and cuffs do not match. History tells us that during times of economic depression, expenditure on hairdressing does not decrease so much as you think it might – this is because it gives at least half the population a vital lift. There lies our absolute justification for not feeling guilty about time spent on our coiffure, especially since there is no need to break the bank – the Superdrug sourced shampoo can leave hair as silky smooth as the Space.NK one. Grooming does not have to cost the earth; if the salon is charging £30 to cut cuticles, do that bit at home, and go for the £6 professional revarnish. Opt for the DIY facial from Superdrug, and with the money saved splurge on a chair massage, something that you could definitely not manage to perform on yourself.

Focus on what makes you feel good in your own body. I like my hands; it is rare that my nails are less than painted perfection. I hate my pale bluish skin, so I am never seen baring flesh without a spray tan – the world does not have to be inflicted with the alternative; my all too good impression of a recently plucked chicken. Feeling good is like a performance-enhancing drug. When I sat my finals, we all turned up looking a mess apart from one girl, who arrived in bohemian glory and glittery eye make-up. We all thought she was mad – those ten minutes she had spent grooming we had spent cramming. When questioned, she just said that she always got better results if she felt good about herself. Glitter Girl was one of the few women to get a first in my subject that year; none of my cramming circle did. Not a day goes by when I do not remember her lesson, and if a confidence boost is required, an extra layer of lip gloss goes on, and a higher heel is worn.

Procedures

There are, of course, options that roam from skin deep to medical territory. With the advent of injections and lasers, the goalposts on what is cosmetic surgery are forever moving, and as it gets ever more advanced and ever more affordable, it is becoming ever more acceptable. Some claim they would never have a facelift while embracing Botox, others have unsightly veins and blemishes lasered whilst making derogatory remarks about anyone who uses injected filler. Both Botox and blemish removal can cost less than an advanced facial. Then there is laser eye surgery, which in the long run is cheaper than contacts and new frames – important health-improving operation or mere vanity project?

It is not about what other people think. Most of the time they will not notice the defects that you do have, or indeed the tricks that you perform to conceal or correct them. However, if you do decide that fixing a flaw will make you feel better and hold your head that much higher, and you can budget for it, then do it. As with any service, make sure you do your research, and only part with your cash for the best.

Timing is key. One schoolfriend of mine with a distinguished nose came back with a small perky one after the summer holidays. Even at the age of 17, she had got it right, but then she was extremely sophisticated and had a mobile phone years before any other contemporary of mine. It is very hard to get work done in your home town without it being noticed afterwards – even if you only nip to the corner shop, news of your every tuck will spread like wildfire, although it is easier when you are single as you have no other half who will get drunk and spill the beans. It can be cheaper to go abroad, but make sure you find a reputable surgeon. One fifty-something SG (well I am not quite sure, she could be anywhere between 40 and 70) regularly disappears to New York to get her skin freshened and veins zapped for less than £200; it would cost double in the UK, and the techniques are not so advanced.

Surgery should always be a last resort as there are serious risks, from a botched op that gives you a trout pout, to landing in intensive care. So do try creams, and in the case of various body parts, exercise first. Personal trainers are always a cheaper fat-burning option than liposuction under a general anaesthetic, and a lesser danger to your person.

Exercise

You have a choice. Every SG can have a flat stomach if they so decide; pregnant people cannot. You can choose not to exercise, but an irritating thing about getting older is that your metabolism will slow down. Exercising means you can still enjoy eating, and the other good news is that fitness is no longer about wearing green gymslips and being picked on during games lessons by bullying girls; you get to do what suits you, in quite fetching sports gear.

There is never any point in setting the exercise bar so high that you will never clamber over it. You need to be realistic about what you can fit in and what activity is right for you. It may be power walking around the park with a dog or your BF; it may be a yoga class where you can gossip with fellow yogi in between downward dogs; it may be biking to work. However, for many a busy SG with an aversion to battling the weather when somewhere warm will perfectly suffice, it will be pounding the treadmill of the gym plugged into your iPod and ignoring the world at large for 40 minutes.

I was always the last to be selected for teams at school owing to my uselessness at everything physical. This put me off such activity for years, but eventually I mustered up the courage to enter the doors of the gym in my early twenties, discovering that by no means was I the most pathetic member, and a few years down the line I bet I can now do more abdominal crunches than anyone in my year.

When joining a gym do not be swayed in your selection by fluffy towels or handsome gym instructors from Commonwealth countries (do you want them to see you at your sweaty worst anyway?). Your gym choice is all about location. I once belonged to a gym 15 minutes' walk away. I struggled in February. I now go to one 30 seconds away and make it, even it is just for 20 minutes, almost every day. The marginally more remote exercise emporium may have been of swisher standard, but was no competition for my bed. Please, if you join such an establishment in January as a result of a New Year's resolution, do not be put off if you have to do battle to use the equipment.

Come February, parents will be back on the school run and the attached's willpower will have fallen through – their partner will have squashed it so they do not feel guilty about doing nothing to alter their own squishy skin.

If you choose a gym attended by no one you know, you can take on an alternative persona. However, if the club is by the office, due care and attention will be called for. I once worked for a record company, and it was compulsory among staff to like indie (cutting edge) music, but I liked my tunes somewhat more fromage-tastic, especially when working out – The Village People being so much easier to feel the burn to than The Verve. We all went to the gym next door, so I used to plug into the club's shared sound system, listen to naff songs on a very naff radio station, and then switch the little box on my treadmill to an indie station before I got off. The one time I forgot, the head of A&R (the department that goes out and sources the talent) got on after me and never forgave me for letting the side down. He even sent a disparaging e-mail about my music choice to my head of department. I got my revenge. Every time I did weights near him, when I was done, I would change the settings so they were far heavier than I would ever bother to push. When he sat down to do them he was suitably freaked out at how superior my skills were. He was also the type that had a favourite cross trainer, which I would try to make sure I beat him to and then spend an inordinate time on so he was forced to use another one.

On entering the gym, all dignity is checked in at the door, and you find yourself in a parallel universe where previously sane people become utter nutters. Indeed, it is somewhat awkward meeting fellow members outside, as people tend to behave so differently – a whole Attenborough wildlife series could be devoted to the various types who inhabit this strange, often subterranean environment.

There are distinct and recognisable species in every gym, and watching these creatures will provide a welcome distraction to your physical exertions. First, we have the cardio princesses, who always use the same cardio machines and never do weights to increase their muscle. Their bodies get so used to the repetition they never lose any weight, and if they ever stop they balloon. As a superior SG you know that to shock your body slim you need to mix up the cardio and turn some of your mass into muscle to quicken your metabolism. Never fear, there is no need to do anything other than remain in the fixed weight area, you do not have to venture into the free weights zone, which always seems to be the exclusive habitat of the weight-lifting hairy monsters. However, if you feel like creating a little havoc, there is nothing like roaming into this arena, especially if you are escorted by an extremely camp gay man and hogging a couple of benches whilst having a noisy chat about the back, sack and crack wax. Suddenly the supposedly red-blooded men around you will start silently sobbing.

In addition to these animals, we have the 'alternative' freaks, who insist on using a skipping rope in an area that causes maximum inconvenience for all concerned before balancing for hours on strange bouncy balls, and at least one obsessive tending on anorexic, who never does classes for fear of a comment about their slim frame. Of course, almost as strange are the people who only do classes, the most serious head-cases of this variety being the body pump people who will arrive hours before the appointed time to set up their equipment near a suitable mirror before then causing themselves an injury because there is no way the instructor can keep an eye on everyone. A few businessmen, who enter the gym's doors to justify long lunches, will bumble along confused that their paunches are not getting any smaller, choosing to forget that this is because they spend all their time in the sauna. There will also be a smattering of scary people with personal trainers along with the scared inductees who, after an instructor has prepared a programme, will probably never darken the doors of the establishment again.

Personal trainers are amazing if you can afford them, but like therapists and friends you need to be picky, so research by asking around in the gym which one will be best for you, and if you do not like the one you choose, change. Girl personal trainers normally work girls harder, and of course you then remove the danger of dealing with any sexual advances, unless they (or you) are of the Martina

Navratilova persuasion. Among my SG circle, a disproportionate number who have employed male trainers have ended up falling for their charms (or perhaps muscly arms is a more accurate take on the circumstances). Indeed, one SG friend, who had taken to incessantly texting her hunky instructor whilst she was away on a boat, caused the suitor who was subsidising the holiday to get so jealous that he dropped her phone into the sea. You are single and therefore free to do what you want, and there is something special about someone finding you attractive when you are at your least, so if the wandering hands add a welcome frisson to your workout, you can go along with it, just be wary of the dangers. When the love affair dies and/or they move to Holmes Place in Harrow, you may find Maltesers and burrowing into your bed for a **Big Duvet** moment a more attractive alternative to the scene of the heartbreak, and although Nestlé might appreciate your state of distress, your hips will not.

Gym locker rooms are bound to make you feel better about your body, as the lighting is so unforgiving it shows up everyone's cellulite. However, there is no need for you to be either a) one of those freaks who has a very complicated dressing routine with their towel wrapped firmly around them fearful of displaying anything (we have all seen it all before) or b) just the opposite, i.e. parading around absolutely starkers. Like everything else in life, think balance!

The Diets

SGs can eat what they want when they want – you are much less likely to be swayed by anyone else's need for munchies and can stock your fridge with what you like. If you are having a proper lunch and only want a chocolate bar for breakfast and cereal for dinner before or after you go out, you can. You do not have another half demanding you cook curry and chips for two.

Of course, if you choose to eat everything that tempts you, you will risk piling on the pounds. Which would not be a problem if you were content being a somewhat bigger beauty, but it then means you are unhealthy, which is. Being too thin can be just as bad – and it shows up wrinkles.

At this point, let us acknowledge a basic fact – diets, whether they be cabbage patch or in the zone, are dull and they make you duller. We all know you are what you eat, that it is all about five portions of fruit and veg a day, that alcohol is full of calories and cake is too. We also know that if you eat less and exercise more you will eventually be slim. It's not rocket science, although the diet industry tries to make out that it is.

If you do diet, do not shout about it, just do it. Fellow females and gay men will often try to sabotage your regime to make them feel less guilty about theirs, whilst straight men will get bored and even annoyed if you refuse to eat. There are invariably lower calorie options, there is always the possibility of meeting people for drinks and not dinner, and then stopping drinking alcohol after the first two glasses (people do not notice after a certain point in the evening whether you are on the lime and soda with or without the vodka).

One SG I know has a maximum weight she is happy in herself with and if she exceeds it, she quietly spends 20 minutes extra on the treadmill during her workouts and has hot mashed up Weetabix either for lunch or dinner. She is back to her comfortable weight within a week. The less difficult you make a diet, the more likely you are to shift those pounds.

Retail Therapy

When you're an SG, you have the privilege of directing your purchasing power to items you feel are essential. Clothes and shoes are your uniform, and if you want to categorise them as the most pressing acquisition to be made, you can. A piquant fact: accessories, for example a cutting-edge handbag swinging from your shoulder, make you interesting – to other women, and to men (gay ones will notice the style, straight ones that you have an innate air of confidence). One newly divorced older SG friend never shopped for herself unless her clothes had fallen apart – her husband made her feel too guilty. He left her; she credits a new handbag with helping her get through some hazardous events solo. And it looks better on her arm than he ever did.

Shoes are spectacular inventions. You can go crazy with them whatever your figure and however much you currently weigh. Thus they are a fairly safe investment, unlike a too-small designer dress that will immediately date. Selecting a shoe can be like selecting a man, just without the emotional trauma, and in the case of my divorced SG friend, cheaper. You can opt for the dull but dependable variety or a sexy one that you know will hurt you before too long, but looks oh-so-good. Plus there's the added bonus that you can walk all over them (in them, at least) and they still come back for more.

If in doubt about your sartorial style, consult any 'Will' you can find. I will never forget arriving, dressed in skin-tight white jeans, cleavage-revealing top and mega platform heels at the office of my most high-powered confirmed bachelor friend (Palace of Westminster power player – I have known this one since birth, he is a friend of my parents) so he could escort me to a party. He looked me up and down, and said, as loudly as possible, so that all the important people (well, politicians and their apparatchiks) in the vicinity could hear, 'It's a bit Liz Hurley, isn't it?' I learnt my lesson. Never feel coerced into being a slave to fashion either, wear what suits you – if you have short legs, sandals with straps that go halfway up them will only accentuate the drawback. If you are prone to being swayed into purchasing errors by pushy shop assistants, take your GBF for protection – they will scuttle off in fear whilst he tells you the truth far better than any mirror or commission brown-noser. They will also encourage you to take justified risks. I once bought an evening dress which I would never have thought I could fit into or get away with wearing until my GBF spotted it whilst rummaging though some racks (I was sitting down having a bored-of-shopping-strop – must stop going on spending sprees in four-inch heels) and manhandled me into it. It is a show-stopper, although he does have to come round to arrange my breasts into it every time I want to wear it out.

Single Holiday

Vital to the SG's vitality is occasionally giving yourself a literal break to keep mind, body and soul in order. Yet another blessing for the SG is that you can take advantage of having more money in the holiday fund, and you are not restricted by school breaks or a partner's preferences. A holiday can be just that, not a 'compromise' trip that will leave you shivering and shattered, and you will thus never be found on a rugby tour in Iceland when you would prefer to be on a beach. Since you have the advantage of being able to go 'out of season' (when school children are in their rightful place, school) you will not have to pay over the odds either. This in turn will make your holiday that much more peaceful – you will not be doing battle with screaming youngsters who cause waves and splash chlorine in your hair every time you get in the peed-in pool.

You can go away with other singles, but select your companions carefully. It is always a good idea to put forward your very specific idea of a perfect holiday while it is in the planning stage – if your friends like running around looking at monuments while your favoured activity is crawling towards a cocktail on the beach, then perhaps you are not compatible break buddies. One SG friend of mine arrived in Ibiza for some gentle sunning and instead was confronted with friends who had metamorphosed into coke-crazed clubbers. If in doubt, and the budget can stretch for it, at least opt for separate rooms.

Perhaps one of the last bastions of bravery for some is the single holiday alone. For this, the spa is perfect, because it will be full of other singles. I have several friends who go out every night at home but then reach the point where they cannot talk to anyone else. They regularly disappear off for pampering at these places so they can become at peace with the world and clamber back on top of it again. Others sometimes declare they have gone away but instead go into hibernation mode at home. They switch off their phones, stock up their fridges and only venture as far as their duvets allow.

The main issue for people thinking about going away alone is dinner. At a spa there will always be an official 'singles' table, but if joining the Joiners fills you with dread, just take a book. However, though you may be feeling anti-social, you may be surprised – you never know who you might meet. One girl I know picked up her husband at such a retreat, whilst I met someone who was to become one of my best financial backers in my work. We almost ended up lovers after meeting quite by chance over a bottle of wine with our spa cuisine one night (we were feeling rebellious – detoxing always makes me want to retox). Then we discovered he knew my father's BF and was also the father of one of my half brother's school friends... Any thoughts of a romantic encounter were swiftly abandoned.

However much we may dream of being away from it all on holiday, all of the time, we do have to go back to reality, and home. Thus we now turn our attention to management of the SG's domestic domain.

Chapter Three

Home Management

Home may be where the heart is if you are a desperate housewife; it has no need to be when you are a content bachelorette.

Instead, where you reside can be whatever you and your bank manager decree it to be – a place only big enough to lay your head, or somewhere to hang out and throw legendary parties in.

Your residence is not about space in the square footage sense, but in the mental one. I have multiple SG friends who live in shoeboxes so small that they would have nowhere to store vast quantities of footwear even if they could afford to buy out Blahnik, and are a hundred times happier. Why? Because as much as they love their parents, they used to live with them. There is a reason girls leave home earlier than boys even though it will stretch them financially just as much – guilt. Yes, again, that emotion which womankind does so well. Since boys fail to notice emotional blackmail as much, they end up on the receiving end of it less – parents just give up giving them grief. Girls thus choose to flee the nest earlier. One Girl Playmate of mine has three lazy brothers, all over the age of 28 and all still living at home; she decamped at 21, but is still the person, after her parents, whom the police would call should the burglar alarm be activated. (Her brothers have been known to sleep through intruder alerts.)

Moving to my own miniature abode and away from living next door to two of my parents gave me one of the best gifts I have ever had: an adult (indeed about as functional as one can get) relationship with them, something that sometimes proved elusive when they could observe – and hear – my every coming and going. Most of my claustrophobia at the set-up was undoubtedly in my own head; however, some of it was justified. Boys coming to visit me were known to sprint down the street in an attempt to avoid the CCTV camera that was trained on my parents' front door, but happened to be positioned at an angle that caught mine too. The

CCTV was wired up to my parents' television set, and I became convinced they sometimes watched their very own 'Big Brother' channel if the only alternative was a rerun of *Neighbours*. One of them had developed a tendency to poke his head out of the kitchen window to say hello to my visitors, and even once called me a dirty stop-out as I tottered home after a night at my then boyfriend's. In his eyes he was, of course, just being friendly, but I minded the lack of privacy and sometimes went out of my way to avoid this pair of parents. When I moved away, they feared the snatched thirty seconds with a grumpy daughter sounding like a monosyllabic teenager would disappear into no contact at all, but the opposite is true – I now see them regularly and properly. Meanwhile, the kitchen-window parent suddenly gained an interest in subscribing to Sky TV soon after I had gone.

The point is, if you can possibly afford to move out, whether renting or buying, it is the best thing you will ever do for your head, if not your bank balance. If it comes down to an either/or scenario, it is absolutely justifiable that your happiness account is healthier than your savings one. Though home does not have to be about where your heart is, it does have to provide you some peace of mind, and having parents on top of you 24/7 when you are no longer a child can be a strain on the relationship and lead to regular clashes. Since my SG friends have left home there have been next to no tears of frustration about the other generation from either side, a stark contrast to the immature comments of the 'you don't respect me' ilk that seemed to abound from both before.

Ideal Home Hunt

First of all, you need to figure out what you want from your abode. There will always be budgetary constraints, but at this point you have fewer people and their agendas – whether they be barbecues and outside space or phenomenally large high-definition television screens – to consider. Space always comes at a premium, and as an SG do you really need that much? Since you are a bachelorette, you can go French – you are young, and free to choose a shabby shoebox for its location rather than somewhere that involves large **Cabbage** (taxi) fares and several empty rooms.

I have lived in my shoebox for over three years, since at the moment my primary requirement is location not largeness. In my SG's world, a good home is somewhere public transport, shops of all description and my working world are on my doorstep. It is a place where I have my own double bed, bathroom and fridge for keeping alcohol and an old lemon in (you can use the latter for detoxing by putting it in hot water, or for adding to G&Ts when you are back in more realistic retox mode). There is no need to feel pressured into domestic goddessry as there is not enough room – I do not possess an ironing board as there is nowhere to put one (I therefore own a lot of lycra-based clothes and, if needs be, place crumpled items in the dryer with a wet flannel for five to ten minutes, which is just as good). I also don't know how to turn on my oven – a fact my mother let slip to my grandmother, who took several moments to recover her celebrated composure at news of this particular granddaughter's ineptitude (my younger female cousin, in contrast, has just got married and has a large eat-in kitchen). Not being fully cognisant of the fundamentals of this cooking appliance really doesn't matter to me; I am an expert microwaver and even know how to turn on my hob. I used to cook when I lived in a house with a dining table; now if anyone comes to dinner we go to the pizza place downstairs as they obviously have lots of tables suitable for eating off whilst I only have one of the coffee variety.

It is all about what makes you happy, which may be feeding the five thousand, in which case you can opt for somewhere larger – although you may also have to purchase hiking boots to get to the bus or train stop – or it could just be a place to pass out in. You may want a wreck to restore or a flawless flat. The important thing is that you feel that your home is your refuge, a place that can rejuvenate you in some way.

Once you have figured out what is important to you, the finance question will loom, and so will the decision on whether to flatmate or not.

Can You Bear to Share?

Whether or not you share may well depend on penny-watching constraints, rather than personal choice. However, if you are in the fortunate position of being able to choose, before you automatically decide to live with someone because it is what you have always done, pause and consider for a moment.

You are no longer a student, when living with people is an essential part of the whole college/university experience, but out in the real world. Being able to walk around naked, eat what you want and mess up the bathroom as much as you like are all perks of being single that no lifetime should be deprived of.

I have been known to wear my coat indoors to cut down on heating bills, rather than put up with a flatmate who would subsidise them, but might mutter about the extravagance. The last straw for one of my SG friends and her ex-flatmate was when she was accused of being exorbitant for buying non-economy toilet roll. They had a screaming row about absorbency and realised it was time they called time on their living arrangements. I have had three flatmates, and although I loved them all dearly, they were no good for my mental health, as I am sure I was dreadful for theirs. I spend too much time having to be 'on' when out, so that I cannot possibly face having a conversation when I am in. When I did live with people this meant they a) got worried about me and never ceased asking if I was all right – very sweet, but very dull having to assure them that I was; or b) were affronted. It was nothing to do with them, I was just all talked out.

One of the major advantages of my minuscule apartment is that there is physically no room for a flatmate, so no one ever asks, and I have no need to say no. One SG friend, who does have a second room, admits its existence can be a trial at times, and she is looking to move to a glitzier one-bedroom. People keep trying to move in or stay with her and then take mortal offence if she turns them down, even when offering her astronomical rent. She works hard for her space and refuses to be swayed by pledges of home-made chocolate-chip cookies or ready-made cleaner on site. Offers of a weekly back massage almost weakened her stance, but she held her ground in the end.

Other SGs I know eschew people for pet company. However, consider carefully before getting a live furry friend. A cat may be the traditional accessory for the SG, but in reality they will require some attention. I deeply miss my feline, Smirnoff, but not his path of night-time destruction that used to greet me every morning. And now he is no longer there the neighbours do not think I am quite the alcoholic they once did as I am not squealing out the name of a vodka brand at breakfast-time. They had no way of knowing it was because my keys had ended up embedded in his litter tray for the umpteenth time. Remember, being an SG is about revelling in your lack of responsibility, not taking it on. Mini canines may well be the accessories *du jour* for the Paris Hiltons of this world, but these four-legged prima donnas are for life, and you probably don't have her entourage to poop-scoop for you if you ever tire of their incongruent capacity to defecate. At least a human being living with you should be toilet-trained.

Of course, for some, having other people pottering around is necessary for their sanity. One SG I know cannot live on her own, and needs her girlfriends to come home to and watch *The OC* with when she has the rare opportunity for a quiet night in. On the other hand, she cannot comprehend my need for utter solitude when I do the same. Whatever your reason for sharing, there are certain pitfalls to avoid, but as long as you are aware of them, you get to share in single life with playmates in tow.

The advantage at this stage of your life is – unlike with your family, who you are landed with – you do get a say in who you live with. When picking someone, think long and hard about whether you really are compatible cohabiting companions, both financially and personally. I could never live with my BF, despite the panic induced into my world if she is out of **Radio Contact** with me for more than a few hours at a time. Financially my BF is out of my league – she is earning far more than I am so can spend more on everything. Not only could this make shared supermarket trips strained, but there is also a discrepancy in outlook with my BF. She is the messiest, laziest, least domesticated person in the world – her dishwasher has been unplugged for over a year, because she just has not got round to getting it installed. (Despite pleas from her long-suffering cleaner.) Even I am not that bad: at least my oven is wired up. We both know we would be utterly incompatible flatmates as I would get far too uptight, but our relationship is secure enough to be able to say that to each other. I do not ever want our friendship to be about who has put out the rubbish – she is far too important to me for that.

Several friends of mine love sharing, as their flatmates are ones that they never see; the set-up of ships passing in the night tends to be a very convenient one. Be wary, however, of living with a friend who has a boyfriend; even the nicest other halves are irritating when you have to talk to them in your pyjamas on a Saturday morning, or scrape their pubic hair off the bath. They are essentially one extra body in a space that cannot accommodate them; loudly snogging on the sofa when you want to watch *The Princess Bride*, or having noisy sex when you need an undisturbed lie-in. These boyfriend creatures are also male, so will have opinions which they opine – on anything from the television channel being watched (and that you are paying for) to your love life, your eating habits or your car. If you do end up an unwitting gooseberry in an unwanted *ménage à trois*, encourage your flatmate to spend a lot of time at his place – if you have to resort to wearing skimpy nightwear at all hours around the flat so she gets slightly concerned about where his eyes are focused then, sometimes, such desperate measures are called for.

Having flatmates is all about boundaries; and if you are clear from the beginning what counts as a breach of these – including the amount of time boyfriends, present and future, can stay for – then domestic delight can still be yours.

The Search

Once you have decided your personal criteria, it is time for the search, whether it be online, through the small ads or via estate agents. A note here: you are an SG, so whatever route you take, keep safety at the forefront of your mind. If you feel remotely uneasy about viewing anything on your own, phone a friend to pootle along with you. They might even be useful – my GBF once prevented me from buying a place by pointing out that it had no storage space for my shoes (I had got rather too carried away by the shiny power shower).

If using agents, contact the ones in the appropriate area and give them your brief. Estate agents, whether you are buying or renting, need to be managed (like everyone you will ever come across).

However, like anyone and everything that needs to be managed, dealing with them is purely a matter of common sense.

First of all, network. Meet as many estate agents as you can, charm them so that if you are buying they are less likely to let their clients gazump you, and, of course, never speak to them without a CL. The CL will be made up of all the things you want and need your home to be, as well as important questions like: 'Who runs the communal areas, how much is the service charge and is it true they are planning to re-route the M25 via the front door?' A few viewings and a couple of episodes of *Location, Location, Location* and you will soon know your freeholds from your leaseholds and how to play your estate agent hand. The only reason I got my shoebox is that the agent called me when the previous buyer had dropped out, and he also stopped another person gazumping me with a higher offer at the last minute by convincing his client I was the more reliable buyer. Being charming works. Despite their reputation, estate agents are surprisingly human, and respond predictably well to buttering up.

Buying on your own can do damage enough to your savings, but surveyors' and lawyers' fees can rub serious salt into the wound. Selecting them is like selecting doctors – do your research and, if you can, ask your friends for recommendations. Both these professions will charge the earth to communicate with you in confusing language, so contrast and compare and make sure that you are at least getting the best deal. And if it turns out you cannot afford to get on the property ladder for now, remember household happiness is about finding a haven to sleep stress-free in.

Bribe friends and relatives to help you pack and move. There is a reason why moving house is considered one of the most stressful things you will ever do. However, the years of peace it should bring you afterwards, not to mention the toned arm muscles from all that carrying and lifting, should make it more than worthwhile.

Your Set-up

So you have the keys, a floor filled with boxes, and a fairly blank canvas. Another advantage of being single is that you can now do whatever you like. You can take forever to unpack, you can decorate as you see fit – the only opinion that matters is your own. Yes, you may have to choose the Argos lemon juicer over Philippe Starck's, but you still have a million decking-out options and no one else sticking their annoying oar in – if there is a flatmate about, it is one you have selected and with whom you are singing from the same hymn sheet.

Home improvements and DIY may be, to you, the most boring tasks imaginable. I certainly think so. However, I do have a pal who spent a year doing up her place on a restricted budget, but has still somehow managed to fill it with shiny fittings and white sofas which small hands won't stain (although there was a somewhat rocky moment in our relationship when there was a slight spillage from my red wine glass over her white carpet. She has since installed a white grape rule, and I now only ever bring bubbles, by way of an apology – she would probably forgive me faster if it was Cristal rather than Cava, but at least I am showing some degree of contrition.) The pristine princess also has black loo roll to match her bathroom's black and white décor, managing to prove the exception to the rule that anything other than white Andrex is tasteless. Another acquaintance has gone for a pink theme – everything from walls to sofas to fridges is, to one degree or another, pink – although her loo roll is still definitely white. The pinkwash is perhaps a reaction to her ex-boyfriend, who previously insisted on all interior decoration in their abode being brown, or sewage-coloured. He was a complete turd to her too; in that relationship's case, the writing was very much on the s**t-coloured walls.

The possibilities when it comes to decorating your dwelling are truly endless. I have one SG friend who has shoes and pashminas in place of adornments, whilst another makes features of coats to brighten up her studio apartment – who needs a painting when you can have a DVF dress coat costing just as much as an imitation Pollock on your wall?

It is a myth that girls do not like gadgets, glistening televisions and sound systems – however, we know that they are not the be all and end all. It is perfectly fine not to possess an encyclopaedic knowledge of the ins and outs of electronics; however, salesmen may consequently see you, the SG, as a soft touch. If you think you will need an expert when out purchasing such items, phone a friend, although pick your authority carefully. I made the mistake of taking my music producer brother shopping with me for these appliances since I thought his knowledge would mean I would not overpay. We ended up having a war of words on Tottenham Court Road, as he was trying to convince me to buy a TV that would not have fitted in my flat, let alone through the door into it.

A note here: measure your doorways before buying beds and sofas. I have had more than one chum unable to get their unrefundable, bargain-in-the-sales king-size bed into their new bedroom, thinking it was a good thing that it wasn't flat-packed so no need to do battle with impossible instructions. The female of the species do not need to give the male variety any extra ammunition on our so-called inability to think practically. Just because our spatial awareness skills may occasionally be less than stellar, that does not mean we are unable to survive without a man and his measuring tape (something an SG should always own anyway, although men for some reason fear us possessing one – can't think why).

Since your home is your private place, especially if you do not have to share, it can be a mess or an utter tribute to good taste. You can take your friends and ask their opinions when homeware shopping, but you do not need to pay any attention to them whatsoever. This is almost always about your private, not your public, persona. If you don't have enough cups and sometimes end up using a jug as a mug, as your humble authoress has done on occasion, who is to know or care?

Considering you are an SG and undoubtedly out and about the majority of days and evenings, the most critical place in your residence is your boudoir, the room where you will spend most time, although admittedly the majority of it will be asleep. The luxury of not having to wage duvet war and being able to fully stretch out over a double bed with a mattress bounce of your choice may well become a savoured memory in later years, so treat this opportunity with respect. Blow your budget and a lot of shopping hours on your bed; it is the most vital thing you will buy. Mine is my most expensive piece of furniture and I was somewhat embarrassed when I bumped into a skinflint friend of mine whilst I was purchasing it. My credit card was having problems going through because it cost so much, and I was terrified she would be derogatory about my extravagance – she has been known to bring a calculator to dinner and quibble over who had bread or not. However, she was very quiet about my acquisition, which I initially put down to her being caught out in a very unfortunate pair of shorts, but eventually found out the real reason when I was round her place some months later: her bed was a more expensive version of mine. Be assured, where you lay your head is a sensible expenditure.

Your boudoir needs to be somewhere you can sleep, and thus it is preferable to keep it peaceful, muted, calm – in colour, decoration and vibe. Yet it is also somewhere to seduce; we may be single, but that does not mean we have the sex life of Maria before she met Captain Von Trapp.

It is a rookie mistake to go back to his place before you have reached the bringing-over-of-a-change-of-clothes stage. Although the sexual revolution has changed many attitudes, the walk of shame is still just that for a female – that panda eye, bed hair, evening outfit look on the trudge to the early morning Tube or, worse still, at work, is simply not a good one. Since a similar journey is still perceived as the strut of pride for a male, if someone wants to kiss you, he should make the effort to come back to yours. You therefore need to feel happy and confident in your bedroom – the sex you have in there will register that much higher on the Richter scale for it.

I speak from experience here; I always have a better time in the boudoir if I have boy-proofed myself and my flat. Usually if a boy is in your bed, you will probably have had some advance warning, and will have your body smooth, all embarrassing products such as depilatory cream hidden from display in the bathroom, and neither grey bras nor granny knickers anywhere in sight in your bedroom. However, life does not always go according to plan, and sometimes you will not have had time to order your habitat.

No man I have ever met really minds the empty tit-tape and control-top tights packets strewn over the floor – their mind is on something else entirely. The second time I was kissing a certain bachelor in my bedroom he remarked how unrecognisable it was compared to the bomb site it had been first time round. The mess had not put him off coming back for more, but on this occasion I had a less inhibited experience with skin more baby- than bear-like and all such paraphernalia out of sight.

If you can afford a cleaner, do not be ashamed nor be an inverse snob about having one – two hours a week helping keep your haven habitable will change your life. You are single, you work hard and you do not always have time to dust the doorknobs. Several of my girlfriends, working very scary hours indeed, have never even met their cleaners whilst, since I often work from home, I know all about the traumas caused by my cleaner's agoraphobia (fear of crowds), acrophobia (heights), amathophobia (dust)... Always buy Christmas presents and leave cash bonuses. As for all circumstances when parting with cash, get personal recommendations for these domestic goddesses, and try not to be like an extremely anal acquaintance of mine who has been known to utter 'Got to go – I have to clean up before the cleaner arrives'. Of course, you should never leave a pigsty for your cleaner, but it is OK to leave them something to do.

Cars

The other massive expenditure in your life other than your abode may well be sitting outside it, whether Porsche or Punto. If you have one, your car will doubtless be your second home, with almost as much make-up and SG clutter in it as your stationary one. Being an SG is about being free – free to flee the parental nest, and also your own. However, if you are an urban girl with some spare cash, do your calculations carefully to make the most of it. One acquaintance sold her ever-depreciating-in-value-and-increasing-in-expenditure vehicle and now hires fun cars – that she could never afford to buy – if she needs to get out of town. She has turned up in a flashy Ferrari at a very dull wedding, and a luxurious Lotus at a university reunion, causing all the males – especially those who had bred and were confined forevermore to large functional vehicles – almost to pass out with jealousy. However, if a car is going to give you more freedom than grief, and you have the cash, then absolutely buy one... but make sure you have a licence first. I know car owners who have not. Seriously.

Once armed with a licence, do not concern yourself with general lack of knowledge in the motoring arena. You will soon pick up what you need to know about things on four wheels and it is actually extremely cool not to recognise your Mercedes from your Mini Coopers. One boy of my acquaintance bought an Aston Martin DB7 for six figures. Two different girls, in the space of 24 hours, genuinely complimented him on his new Ford Probe. He sold the Aston at a massive loss soon afterwards, this particular vanity project not providing the James Bond pulling power he had hoped from it.

If you are going to buy a car, the steps that you need to take are exactly the same as dealing with anyone else you require a service from. Research the best places to purchase and cross-check your findings with friends. It is probably best to buy second-hand, even if only by a few months, as nothing loses value so quickly as a an automobile. Only ever talk with a dealer (preferably one outside town – they tend to offer better prices) armed with a CL comprised of questions gleaned from the Net, *Top Gear* and friends in the know, and consult more than one vendor so you can make an informed decision. It has been proven that women pay more for cars than men do, which is distinctly unfair, so when you buy take a Wingman with you to ensure that the only ride you are taking is in your latest acquisition. All these rules apply when servicing and selling too.

This is your chance, again, to get what you want within your budget. You do not have to squeeze in squealing toddlers, stroppy teenagers, or stout spouses. Who said a customised pink Mini Cooper wasn't a rational choice for the road? You have the rest of your life to be sensible. If it is your lifetime ambition to own a soft top, and your bank manager says OK, then why not? It says a lot about the hopefulness of the average Briton that the UK has more soft tops per capita than any other European nation, despite the climate being so much more dreadful than so many countries on the Continent, and the car crime rate just as high. If you want extra lipstick mirrors that light up (best *not* whilst in motion, please, SGs), or to opt for a better looking dashboard, then it is your prerogative. You are allowed Sat Nav; it is not like you cannot read a map or are not willing to ask people for directions like the male species, it just may not always be safe to stop and ask. (So there, boys.)

Too many gadgets, however, can be distracting. I know an SG who bought a device to help with her parking, but when it went off to indicate she was too close to the car behind she thought it was her mobile ringing and ignored it. There was an expensive prang. It is a cliché that girls cannot park, and admittedly one I and my gadget-loving friend live up to, but my mother is the best parker I know (which my ex-stepfather always got hugely irritated by). It is a proven fact, backed up by insurance companies who would never do anything to risk their profits, that women are superior, safer drivers. We have better judgement. Full stop.

Chapter Four

Family Management

Everyone is an expert on families – other people's, that is.

We can all comment with great insight on those we read about in *Heat* or *Hello!*, tut-tutting over a film star's exploits with the nanny or the Royal Family's Christmas gathering guest list. We will provide a shrewd perspective for those in our acquaintance on how they should be interacting with their relatives. When it comes to our own, however, it will almost always be a different story.

There is a wise old Chinese saying: 'Govern a family as you would cook a small fish – very gently.' The subtlety and sensitivity everyone needs when managing their worlds is never more vital than in their dealings with family, and this is especially true for SGs.

For every SG I know, family is the cornerstone of their very being (it has to be – they have no partner or child to take that role), and is the most complex set of relationships they have to cope with. Family makes them laugh – and cry – harder than anyone else in their SG world. All of my SG friends and I have found it impossible to get it right with relatives all the time, especially in the twenty-first century where the make-up of most families is getting ever more complicated courtesy of a divorce rate at almost one in two.

Relative Values

The SG has her own specific challenges when it comes to kith and kin. Because she is single, to some older generations she can be perceived as being in a semi-childlike twilight zone. The SG generation is something new for society to deal with, so there is no reason for our families to know how to treat us. There are manuals on nappy changing and rebellious teenagers, not on how to deal with an SG living and loving her lifestyle.

In the past, you became an adult when you got married and had children or you were a spinster and a burden. Children may now lose their innocence earlier, but they also tend to be in education and single longer – so when do they become adult? The SG specifically provides further anxiety, and for parents in particular. Having an available daughter of marriageable age is traditionally a worry for her mother and father. In the back of parents' minds, programmed through centuries, is the thought that such a daughter cannot possibly be fulfilled, because she is still single. Until you get to grips with your relatives' concern about your SG status, it may mean you are still considered in childlike terms and are thus on the receiving end of much more 'advice' than attached family members of a similar age.

If you are anything like my SG friends, your familial relations will bear more resemblance to the Simpsons than those of the Partridge variety – blood seems all too liable to take offence when none is meant. One SG wept buckets after her graphic designer dad thought it hilarious to mock up an alternative poster of the film *Single White Female.* He used her picture instead of the leading lady's, and changed the title to *Single Woman Failure.*

Neither party in this state of affairs was acting like a grown-up. Indeed it is a rite of passage to realise that however much you age, you are likely, on some level, not to feel grown-up at all: you finally comprehend that this is the mindset the older generations in your world must have as well. No one has, or ever can have, all the answers, and every age group has their own challenges. Older ones find their health is on the front line and more of their friends are permanently disappearing and, sadly, in the modern era, perhaps their marriages collapsing.

For SGs, in particular, it is only natural to want your family's approval – you love them more than anything, and so their opinions matter more than anyone's. But it is hard. All family wants is for you to be happy. Unfortunately, nobody is going to be completely happy all the time – the best anyone can hope for is mostly happy most of the time. As an SG, your relatives will worry that you are intrinsically unhappy, and the situation will become a vicious circle, since the burden of their concern will be making you downcast too. The time has come for the SG to manage the troops off the M25 and back onto the straight and narrow of a Roman Road. Wearing an elegant Russell Crowesque skirt, naturally.

Manage Expectations

The first fundamental step in good family management for many an SG will be to handle their relatives' expectations effectively. We already know that leaving home is a giant leap towards an adult relationship with the parents. Just make sure you leave the Miss Goody Two Shoes act behind along with the boy band posters and matching duvet, since it will probably get you nowhere. An SG friend of mine always cleans the kitchen before anyone wakes on a Sunday morning when she visits the parental household. There are never any thank yous forthcoming, but when her brother once did it he got the iPod he had been lusting after. You may find that sometimes your family will endeavour to be indirect when trying to place the onus on you, but their methods will usually be about as subtle as a sledgehammer. The same SG's father once called her to ask her if she thought her irresponsible brother could bake a cake for their mother's birthday, which was an obvious ploy to guilt trip a girl who works 24/7 into making it. So she did, but seethed at the way she was expected to – if her dad had just come out and said he would like her to do it in the first place, she would have happily done so. Instead, there was a wasted ten minute conversation in the middle of a manic working day when she was just wound up by how useless her brother was, and how she was always having to pick up the pieces.

I am not advocating becoming a lazy and insensitive person, but just inserting some boundaries if your relatives are running you ragged. The more you accept family guilt trips, the more you will be subject to. These never serve anyone – the SGs end up feeling doghouse deserving, whilst their relatives convince themselves they are so neglected that they are one paw away from Battersea Dogs Home. Families are not just for Christmas (thank God), but for life.

Therefore to become a happy SG, you may have to acknowledge that you will never wholly please your family, your parents in particular. You may never see or do enough for them. Many of my friends find their relatives contrary at times – if they are successful in their career they will be working too hard; if they are not, then they are a disappointment. As they do not have a boyfriend there is the fear, sometimes voiced but continually implied, that they are on the shelf, leaving it too late and may never have babies – never mind that they might not actually want them. Of course, whenever they have had a boyfriend there was something wrong with him.

Once you have come to terms with the fact that it is impossible to completely delight them, life – and family guilt – becomes a lot easier to bear. If this is your story, you need to recognise you should take a step back and make interaction with your relatives work better for you and, although they may not always realise or relish it at the time, for them as well.

As outlined previously, being indirect in areas such as your working world can reap rewards; this will not be the case in your familial one. As an SG, they may regard you as being more at their beck and call than any other attached or unreliable (male) relatives. You may need to train your families to actually ask for what they want by ignoring any veiled requests, and refusing to act until they spell it out. Your family may consider more carefully whether it is really reasonable for you to be carrying out the duty and if someone else should be pulling their weight. This could reduce your daughterly burden to a fair level. What is more, you will know exactly what help they want. One SG I know was driven to distraction by her grandmother, who had just had a fall, because she was getting mixed messages about how she wanted the aftercare to be structured. They had never had a transparent relationship – every entreaty was hidden in some way, which subsequently caused serious problems when her grandmother would have preferred to be in her own home recuperating and watching *Countdown* in peace, rather than at her cousin's, rowing over the conundrum. Emotional guilt tripping serves neither you nor them, it just builds unhealthy resentment – there is no need for anyone to be a martyr. A family full of quasi-saints on the surface only ever results in devilish demeanours lurking underneath.

Friends have found that if they ensure their relatives do not expect too much, they are not such a disappointment and their achievements are a pleasant and appreciated surprise. I know a girl who left Cambridge with a double first, tried her hand in a top advertising firm, and then gave it all up to become a gardener. Her social mountaineering parents (they are too advanced to be called climbers) could not understand – what was their high flyer, whom they used to boast about to all their friends, doing? It got to the stage where the parents tried to manhandle their daughter into therapy. However, she just happens to like gardening and is far happier than many 'professional' people.

Many family members just cannot tell you that they are proud, but underneath it all, they undoubtedly are. Gardening girl's parents eventually saw she had taken the right path for her, and ever since the environment became the fashionable cause *du jour*, they wheel her out at all the fundraising events they attend for Africa/Asia/ Aylesbury town centre's allotment project.

To return to the issue of establishing boundaries, there is the eminently pertinent example of one confidant of mine. This SG spent so much of her time trying to please her parents – about as easy a task as eating a donut without licking your lips – that they distressed and dazed her into therapy. The therapist made her see that she needed to stop being affected by their agendas so much, and her parents in turn realised they needed to leave their loved one to her own devices a considerable amount more. She subsequently got the job, body (healthy state of mind – and weight) and home she, not they, sought, and her life back on track – which was all everyone wanted. Only by running your SG lives yourselves, encouraging your relatives to relinquish the task if they still consider it theirs, will you be at peace. Some older family members may struggle with the concept; after all, they used to wipe your bottom (or got someone they married or paid or both to do it), but they need to come to terms with it all the same, for everyone's sanity.

Of course it is important to listen to your family, but it is just as vital to realise you do not have to accept everything they say any more, and you will have to find a way to make that point to them. One SG friend had an older married sister who was especially strident in her views about which career path her sibling should take – actress or accountant. The SG was initially upset at the interference, but then took a step back, saw the situation for what it was, her sister's concern, and also how to stop the onslaught. The SG reminded her older and supposedly wiser sibling of the time that she herself had moved to Amsterdam to run a 'café', much to their family's extremely vocal chagrin. She went ahead anyway – and married a Dutch merchant b(w)anker whom she met whilst serving 'cake'. Big sis, now Mrs Conventionalist entrenched in a *Vicar of Dibley*-esque abode, was forced to bite her tongue.

Family members of your own generation will understand more about where you are coming from and going to than anyone else on this earth – I would be lost without my rock of a brother – and they should be your allies. So make them that way. I have seen my friends tie themselves in jealous knots over their siblings – driven to distraction by their better looks or bigger bank balance. One SG I know has never got over the fact that her brother will get the business and the flat above the shop when their dad retires. The bitterness simply tears her apart – despite the fact that it is a car-repair garage, and as her car insurance company would vouch for, she does not know the difference between reverse and first gear. Apparently, it is the principle. The SGs who have found peace with themselves are the ones who have accepted that it is not their siblings' fault if their parents have spent more time or money on them, and still play with them anyway – although play now more often means clubbing than Connect Four. Resentment is hard to bear – and can cause unsightly furrowed brows that can only be fixed by costly cosmetic procedures draining money better spent on footwear.

You are your own person. Following your family's every word of advice may not make you any happier; yet occasionally bearing some of it in mind can. This point in your SG life is about nourishing yourself into flourishing. You are a woman in your prime – so seize the day. Some of the decisions you take in life may not be straightforward, but then life itself is about as easy as walking in a straight line in oversized Louboutins.

It is astounding what experts relatives can be in all aspects of your life if you let them. Sometimes they will be helpful, and come up with career-making suggestions, and other times they will get it wrong. Two of mine were bemused that I turned down ITV1's *Love Island* to write this book. I can only hope my decision is proven right in the end! Of course on other occasions, they have been absolutely correct about the path I should follow. It is always unwise to take anyone else's view as gospel, whether they be friend, foe or relative; at the end of the day it has to be your decision, as you are the one who will have to live with it.

Familial Encounters

Real-life visits or encounters need to be a regular occurrence, but not routine, so relatives are not reduced to an apoplectic state if you change the plan because something else vital has cropped up in your SG world. They need to know that just because you do not have a partner and/or child you do still have responsibilities – but one of your responsibilities is to help them realise this. The older generations of your family will not be around forever, and you do love them to bits – but if they are leaving you in bits this is a problem, so take steps to prevent it.

My SG friends have thus learnt the art of backtracking. For example, they offer to visit, and the relatives complain that it is not for long enough; they then say they unfortunately will not be able to come at all; finally, the relatives agree to the initial offer. If their families are being utterly unreasonable then they sometimes throw a sickie and do not even pitch up.

Some relatives may see life as a competition and, from men to careers to weight, they compare you to both themselves and your contemporaries, whether relatives or early achievers the media have unhelpfully featured. One SG friend, an ex-anorexic, read in her mother's Christmas round robin how she was pleased to report that after 30 years of happy marriage she was still slimmer than both her twenty-something, single daughters. Round robins should be banned, they are like New Year's Resolutions in creating unnecessary pressure to 'achieve' – although it would leave my mum and myself bereft of our annual wine bottle sharing ritual, where we weep with laughter over the self-applauding anecdotes of the Cathcarts and Worthington-Smiths (pronounced Smythe, don't you know). If you feel your relatives are putting you down in such unfair and unrefined fashion, consider for a moment why they are lashing out like this. It will be more about their shortcomings than yours – Mrs Round Robin was a desperate housewife hysterical about turning fifty and the thought of middle age and its spread. Such criticism, well-meaning or not, should not set you on a depressing downward spiral, hence it is vital that you come to terms with your own body beautiful.

You may find yourself under an occasional but heart-in-right-place offensive from your family. If you are en route to a scheduled encounter and think you are in danger of undergoing such friendly fire, make sure you have a CL in reserve, with retorts ready about career, men and lack of grandchildren. The CL may not always be necessary, but it might be invaluable if your relatives know how to pick their moments. I have one German confidant who has a perfectly reasonable relationship with her parents until they all get in a car, at which point, whilst squeezed in the back with her two small half-siblings and two over-sized canines, her super-successful solicitor of a stepmother takes control of the wheel and the conversation. Without a CL, my friend inevitably falls to pieces, regressing to pre-pubescent powerlessness as her father sits in the front making supportive noises to his wife. Until their offspring start going off the rails and taking the pressure off her, the CL is the only way my friend has any chance of seizing the conductor's role from her stepmother and orchestrating the conversation to something guaranteed to keep her strops at bay.

Arguments heated by the passion of blood rarely do anyone any good, so are best avoided before they are started. Steering a familial encounter towards sweetness and light is a tactic all SGs need to master, and there are some general topics for the CL that should ensure everyone has a convivial time.

First of all, catch up on 'news', aka gossip, and ask about them, their friends, and your relatives. Relatives, although they often deny it, love 'news'; one friend's aunt positively revels in 'bad news'. You may not know the second cousin they are talking about, but pretend you do and go with the diversion. Health is an exceptionally safe topic – they can bang on about theirs and other people's for hours.

Such diversionary manoeuvres will have to end eventually, however, so when the topic turns to you, you may need to edit your contribution to keep things on a positive note. In your career, there is never a crisis, even if you have been fired – it is a good thing, just a repositioning. It may serve you well to be wary when revealing to them the existence of any Distractions of the male variety; relatives can get slightly ahead of themselves and start shopping for a hat or composing a wedding speech. They could also take it upon themselves to do some more research. One SG friend of mine was kissing a chef who worked in a restaurant near the family home. Her father considers himself something of a wit, so dined there and sent such cryptic compliments to the chef that he came out to converse with the client. It was the wrong chef – but her father did not realise until he had almost had a coronary over the number of tattoos the young man had.

However content you are, the fundamental problem, in many a relative's eye, of their SG relation is that she is single, so sometimes they will try to help, with varying degrees of disaster. The problem is, if they were part of the swinging sixties and seventies generations, they think they are on your wavelength. One acquaintance of mine was sat down aged 21 by her mother and told that some women make good wives, some women make good lovers and had she made up her mind about which one she was going to be? Apparently she could not be both. Her mother, incidentally, had opted for the lover option and the associated complications of having three children by three different men on three different continents (although that is where the semblance with Madonna ends). Another's spends every conversation with her daughter speculating over whom she might marry, to the extent she goes through *Tatler's* Little Black Book of eligible bachelors every year with a highlighter pen. Her daughter is 23, hardly anywhere near a shelf, and with a burgeoning career as a merchant banker.

Relatives like to play cupid. This is normally futile – however, do not completely dismiss the idea out of court if you decide you might like a male Object to dally with. The love of my life (so far) resulted from my parents sitting me next to the gentleman at dinner. Never expect anything from such matchmaking, but your friends and family do know you and thus sometimes get it right. Not always, naturally. One of my Genuine Girlfiends in New York was sent on a date set up by both sets of parents, with a man whom she instantly realised was gay. They became best friends, and she was there for him when he finally plucked up the courage to come out to his family. Some SGs I know stand accused by their relatives of being too fussy, but of course, not as fussy as they would be if they brought home an obese wastrel with an IQ of 22. One of my schoolfriends actually brought home such a specimen when her parents became too impossible on the boy topic. They have not asked about her love life since, learning that information is rationed as a reward for good behaviour – the more they pry the less they get, but the less they interfere the more she may choose to share with them.

Ultimately, you will have to deal with role reversal, and there will come a time when you have to raise awkward issues with the older generations. Sometimes this will manifest itself as advice – one

SG lawyer acquaintance has prevented her somewhat fickle father from entering his fourth marital union without a pre-nup, saving him considerable sums. Other times it will be as you take on the carer role. Always do it kindly – upstart youngsters telling an older family member, 'you need to stop driving, you are a danger to society' will be a massive blow. You could use Bunbury's older, slightly batty, relative at this point as a good way to approach the problem, claiming that he or she almost ran over a small child, and seek your family member's advice on what Bunbury should do to stop their reckless relative driving. My friends report that this tactic often helps their relatives realise, of their own accord, that they should take heed and apply the advice to their own situation.

Tasks

Criticising your family should be your final resort, as the last thing you really want to do is make any of them feel bad. It is important to acknowledge that they just like to feel useful – sometimes it is their fear that they are surplus to requirements that can make them misbehave. The SG may not have supplied children to be fussed over, however they do have other ways of making family feel wanted.

Give your relatives tasks: select jobs that they want to do, and you do not, or cannot do, but which need to be done. These include sewing, DIY, car advice and nursing you through ill health. Grant family a purpose, and even though they may mention your shortcomings in not being able to do the job, they will complete the chore for you. I went into hospital to have laser eye surgery and had to allocate aftercare to a parent. (There was even a competition over which one would get to look after me – parents can be great!) My chosen parent – my mum, as mums are better even than boyfriends (if you have ever had to deal with a boyfriend's impersonation of nursemaid, you will appreciate where I am coming from) – luxuriated in the fact that she was needed. What could have taken a few minutes in planning – collecting me from the hospital and driving me home – she spent several weeks arranging. I was whisked back to my flat, given a beautiful bunch of flowers, had my eye drops applied, was tucked up in bed, and had regular calls as to my well-being for weeks. I felt very much loved. And so, I suspect, did she.

If I am ditched, the first person I call is my father. He promptly takes me out to dinner *à deux* and gazes at me adoringly across the table (causing some less salubrious, not to mention slack, hacks to speculate he has a new 'mystery blonde' in his life – perhaps my hair colour expenditure has been a little high lately), unable to comprehend how any man could not love me. There is nothing like a father's adoration at this low SG point – no man will ever love me as much or think I am as beautiful as my dad does.

If you keep your relationship with your family busy, you can enjoy each other. Borrow things from them. Grandparents have useful stockpiles of things like wheelie suitcases in every conceivable size – baggage that you actually want them to give you.

If you have a family member who, for whatever reason, finds themselves alone, arrange to do fun things with them whilst encouraging them to build up a support network of their own friends – you cannot fulfil this role for them, you are their relative, not their best bud. One SG friend of mine's mother was deserted by her stepfather. After initially ensuring everyone got a fair deal with the minimum use of lawyers with their unsavoury tendency to haemorrhage their clients' cash, the SG then set about schooling her mum in the SG ropes. The daughter rarely agreed to rendezvous with her mum at home for close to two years; instead she helped rebuild the shattered older woman's confidence by luring her out to increasingly glamorous places, so she was enticed to leave the house and get dressed up. When they went on holiday together it was for makeovers on spa breaks. The tough love worked; now a much happier pupil outspends the mistress on shoes, and has just as hectic a social life. Mother and daughter even both recently bumped into each other in a nightclub, and were eyed up by the same group of 25-year-old males. Mummy even had a rather yummy time with one of them.

You do love each other, and it would be a heartbreaking loss if you avoided each other so long that you regretted it in the end.

With a little management, a healthy and happy relationship with every member of your family can be yours. But nowhere will your patience and management techniques be more tested than over that annual testing ground. The festive season, which for so many, is anything but.

The Festive Season Survival Section

More people end up in Relate and divorce lawyers' offices in January than at any other time of the year, and with good reason. Whether it be Christmas or Hanukkah (or indeed *The OC*'s Seth's Chrismukkah) followed by New Year's Eve, for some families it can be a seriously challenging experience. Human beings are contrary souls, and if it is compulsory to have a good time, we invariably do not, added to which, you have to spend time with people you do not normally choose to. If you love the festive season, fine, skip this section, but most people have traumas dealing with their families, especially SGs who are crammed into single beds and are given mournful looks because they have not supplied the proceedings with over-tired, obnoxious brats to give everyone earache.

We will begin with a happy thought, even if you are allocated a 5ft by 2ft bed. You do not have any in-laws and thus you are not multiplying the family management needed; a mother-in-law, so I understand, can be the ultimate nightmare.

The problem with Christmas for SGs is that it is all about family and children. The family she has got are probably indulging in toddler-like tantrums, whilst she will have no pipsqueaks of her own demanding Mum join in the excitement about how Santa drank *all* the whisky left out for him, although Rudolph seemed to be off his carrots. Compounding the situation is that the SG has reached a stage in life where her relatives have had at least two decades to nurture an obsession with tradition that can scale quite scary proportions. There is a routine that must be adhered to, and if it is broken, mass offence occurs. I know of one father who sulks if everyone is not up by 7.30 a.m., in church by 8.30 a.m., and in front of the Queen by 3 p.m. – and heaven forbid if anyone opens a present before lunch. Of course, he does not actually do any of the wrapping or present buying, although he does make a great show of using every pan in the kitchen to make the bread sauce, whilst everyone around him reaches boiling point at his rigid behaviour. Live a little – does it really matter if you open all your presents before breakfast and use an OXO cube for the gravy? No, so fight back. Once you hit adulthood, start to suggest breaking with tradition; from Christmas dinner in a restaurant to spending Yuletide out of the country.

The ultimate break with tradition is by far the best option for the SG – why not put everyone's noses out of joint and just not turn up at all? Your stiletto boots are made for walking (well, taking very small steps to the nearest Cabbage at least) and will be wasted on the company of people force-feeding you Cruciferae. Why do you have to spend Christmas freezing in a cramped space alongside grumpy souls with only cold drizzle outside to escape to? A benefit of being single is being able to think outside the box. Spending Christmas with your friends – the family you choose – is becoming an important milestone to adulthood. You love your family, you make the effort to spend quality time with them the rest of the year, but Christmas is the only time when the majority of work stops, so you must take advantage of the break. I have one friend who runs her own advertising business and Christmas is the only time she can get away. Her mother has been trained to cope without her at Christmas, and to make the most of spa weekends with her daughter the rest of the year.

Aged 25, my BF and I had had a very tough year, culminating in both of us being ditched by men we had really loved. Neither of us could face a Christmas looking at noisily attached loved-up younger relatives. Instead, to recuperate, we escaped to a cottage in Norfolk so remote that we had no mobile reception apart from up a sand dune, on which we precariously balanced to phone various homes on Christmas day. I will never forget skipping along the beach after we had watched *Ferris Bueller's Day Off* and feasted on salmon (for me) and steak (for her) and watching all the sullen families get some air. We returned revitalised, refreshed, and our unexpected presence at family Christmases ever since has been that much more appreciated.

You may even choose to spend Christmas alone. As a single person, you are liable to be out far more than the attached – my single friends and I often find ourselves out every night of the week – partly work, partly fun. In December, excursions become especially intensive for the single soul, so by the holy day itself, you just want to stop talking. One SG friend has no choice; she has invariably over-done it in weeks previous to the extent that by Christmas she has lost her voice, and is usually bed-ridden with bronchitis for most of it. Christmas is an event for people who do not go out as much as your average SG.

However, if you do decide to **Not F**king Invite (NFI)** *anyone* to your 25 December, you may have to get very determined – nay stubborn – to get away with it (perhaps even resorting to telling everyone you are spending it with Bunbury). Alternatively I have several friends who work for charities over Christmas; no one should ever behave so badly as to complain about someone's absence for this reason, and if so they can be firmly, and swiftly, put in their place.

Part of the problem of absconding from Christmas is that relatives can interpret this as not being valued. They are. Give plenty of advance notice and then hold your nerve. You are not destroying the family unit; indeed, suggest that everyone also goes away on holiday. They may, begrudgingly, thank you for it come January. Ignore woeful comments about the prospect of your absence ('but who will untangle the fairy lights now?'). Instead, every time one is made counter with a happy one: 'It's so great you're being so understanding about me going away, not like Bunbury's relatives, it makes such a difference us having such an adult relationship' etc. etc.

Arrange to see your family properly another time in January when there is nothing and nobody to do anyway, and when the mood destroyers (alcohol and caffeine) are not so prevalent, and send them really good presents.

Presents, of course, are another minefield, especially for the SG unable to give joint ones thereby sharing costs and labour. Not for nothing is Santa an anagram of Satan. The legendary row between Van Gogh and fellow painter Gauguin, during which the former sliced off his ear and gave it to a lady friend, took place at Christmas. At least your unwanted presents are never *that* bad.

There are some silver linings in the Christmas clouds for the SG, for at least you will not have to share with a partner or entire family, even if all you receive is a hamper containing such gastronomic delights as cherry brandy and blue cheese mayonnaise. However, to make sure you really reap the benefits of receiving your own presents, implement present lists. Exchange them with your relatives. Even maintain a Christmas book in which you note down every year what you have given everyone so there is never any (unplanned) present repetition. The Internet is your friend (in November, not in December, when packages tend to get delayed and will cause you to arrive presentless, almost always for little people who will then start sobbing). Use it. Most of my SG friends now do eighty per cent of their shopping online; it involves minimum effort, maximum amount of tea drinking. And they also now give better presents and blow less better-spent-on-clutch-bags cash, as they sit and calmly think about what to buy, rather than get furious in crowds and make rash, extravagant selections.

Keep your own present list limited to useful things that relatives know how to purchase, like saucepans and suitcases, and that cannot be used as ammunition against your SG lifestyle. Requests for Ann Summers vouchers, even if they are bestowed, will no doubt be sniped about whilst the turkey (the most boring meat in existence) has to go back into the oven for another three hours because it is still as bloody as everyone's moods. You can never be too specific. One friend of mine asked for a small black umbrella as she was always losing hers – she got a small black umbrella with 'interesting' patterns. She has still got the umbrella, but would rather go Miss Wet T-shirt in front of a building site than use the unsightly thing.

On receiving presents, never raise your hopes too high, and attempt to develop a thick skin against any perceived SG slights.

One daughter I know received in three successive years as her only presents from her frugal mother: a grunge coloured flannel, an orange plastic bookend, and then, when the younger woman had been recently ditched by her long-term partner, a teapot-for-one so minute it would not even provide a small cuppa.

For those SGs who feel reluctant but duty-bound to attend the family Christmas, acquire a bunker mentality, and just keep in mind that you only have to do it once a year. My SG posse are exponents of the survival strategies of both amused detachment and taking perverse pleasure in any hideousness that might arise. If you are really concerned about how it will go, strictly limit the time you spend *en famille*, arriving late and leaving early, and if possible drive, so you have an escape route. Encourage random people to attend – the more the merrier. Randoms can be invaluable, as they tend to act as a buffer and make everyone behave better and not regress to childhood stereotypes. But do watch whom you invite. One girlfriend of mine, who had finally, on her thirtieth birthday (which falls at Christmas), convinced her family to break with convention and do Yuletide abroad in Morocco, brought a schoolfriend along, who had known the family since she was 11. The friend decided to bed her host's little brother, and they spent the trip holding hands and having noisy sex, keeping everyone in their villa awake.

It is probably prudent for you to prepare a lengthy CL for the duration and purchase good presents. I am the Christmas stocking queen, making sure all females in the family get fabulous ones (men for some reason are incapable of sourcing satsumas and bubble bath). Keep your (and other people's) level of alcohol ticking over so it takes the edge off, and allows you to block out anything you do not want to hear. Take charge of handing around the canapés if you want to reduce time spent actually conversing and encourage excursions, even if they are only to the village shop. Selflessly lose at board games if you can possibly manage it. From your friends' texts you know (unless they went away) that no one is having a better time than you.

Go home, write your thank you letters, and use any remaining credit on your card to pre-book your trip to somewhere away from it all next year. Family can usually be managed, and your relationship be a good one, but Christmas can test the skills of any expert.

We now move to the family you choose. Your friends.

Chapter Five

Friend Management

Friends make the world go round; they are an essential part of balanced living and being, especially when you are single.

They are the family you get to pick; your playmates when you want to have fun, your support network when you are down, your DIY helpers who will also pick up their virtual tools whenever you are in need of fixing.

Your friends will always be there for you; it may be an American sitcom cliché, but that is why Jennifer Aniston is such a squillionaire. I have lost count of the number of couples I know who lead such insular lives that it causes their relationships to implode – and then they find they have to rebuild their network of friends because they neglected them so, at the very moment when they need them most. You are single, you have the time to lavish attention on your friends. You are also not kissing them – if you are, lines have been crossed, definitions changed and that is a matter for later chapters – and thus unlike lovers, who can so often be the cause of problems to begin with, they are not going to desert you in times of distress.

A bona fide confidant will hang on in there with you when bosses, doctors, men and relatives are pushing you over the edge. It can be at the most unexpected times where friends' assistance is unparalleled. One SG found herself pulling off a minor miracle in feeding-the-five-thousand fashion for her grandparents' thirtieth anniversary of their pub opening. There were crossed wires over numbers; she thought her grandmother said in her lilting Irish tones that 'four to five' of the family's friends plus the extended clan of traditional Irish proportions had been invited, not the 45 acquaintances as well as relatives actually guest-listed. The loaves and fishes routine was put into jeopardy by the SG's brothers and cousins who, instead of following the FHB (family hold back) rule as beseeched, decided to stack their plates sky high. The party was in dire danger of a cocktail sausage shortage, but the SG's BF since birth (hence always invited) rescued the situation, even rushing out mid-Riverdance to Sainsbury's. Friends succeed in their support because they are that much more in tune with you, their awareness and acknowledgement skills superior to that of your kin – in this instance the SG's BF registered she was stressed, listened to how she could help, and acted accordingly.

There are, of course, different types of friends, with varying degrees of closeness. As an SG it is vital to have in your world people whom you do not have to walk on eggshells with, to whom you can say anything, who because your friendship runs so deep will never judge you even when you are being mean or irrational.

There cannot, by definition, be that many eggshell-free friends – the degree of intensity to the relationship is just too great to maintain with a vast number of people. There will be others whose own insecurity means you have to think a little more around them, and newer friends, who you are just starting out with. However, friendship is something that should not require time you really resent giving, and if it does, you need to re-evaluate these people's involvement in your world. Friendships should be voluntary, not compulsory, that is their wonder.

To attain maximum enjoyment of your SG life and ensure that it is sufficiently spiced up, it is essential to have extensive variety to your playlist of friends. We shall now turn our attention to these, before moving on to how to acquire and nurture them.

The foundation of your SG's world will be your Genuine Girlfriends. You can say the unsayable to these gorgeous girls, who know you are lovely really, and if you are having a rant they will either concur with you and join in, or steer you back on to the right and reasonable path. These girls are the ones you can go out for cocktails with, safe in the knowledge that however many you imbibe, the cock-tales told will go no further. Furthermore, Genuine Girlfriends, unlike their less trustworthy counterparts – girls who may not necessarily always have your best interests at heart, although they will certainly have theirs – should faithfully adhere to the 'girls' code' of behaviour – specifically not kissing each other's exes or befriending these men when they should be ostracised.

Some of your Genuine Girlfriends may change along with your circumstances, but there will undoubtedly be constants throughout your life whom you would be lost without, and probably one in particular – your BF. I have known my BF since I was 11 and she knows more about me than I do. She has a grown-up job compared to my fluffy ones, so lives a completely different life to me and as such we rarely see each other – but our outlook is the same, we speak at least twice a day, about anything and everything. She understands the way my relatives tick, so gives invaluable advice in managing them, and is so in tune with me that I can call her up from a restaurant and ask her what pudding I want and she will tell me.

There is a reason why every legendary fictional SG who appears on the screen or in print (Grace, Bridget, Carrie) has a GBF. It is because if you can find one, they will become more important to your SG's existence than a lung, being as they are always bitchier, sluttier and hairier than you. I have known mine since graduation and we are inseparable despite an unfortunate incident on the night we met when, after one too many vodkas, he put me on a night bus to Penge (instead of Paddington), which I am not sure is even in London (it is certainly not somewhere **Little Black Buses** will venture). With my GBF I can be as impertinent as I like about people in my world and he will be ruder, if I have been naughty with a boy he will have behaved ten times worse with ten times as many, and he will also be unstintingly honest about my looks, telling me without reservation if it is time for me to undergo some procedures.

Much of the SG's life is about the quest for balance, and thus to many an SG, a **Straight and Male Best Friend** (**S&MBF**) is eminently helpful. The outside world may think you are actually kissing or are destined to end up together – one SG friend's parents are convinced she is going to marry hers, even though she has more sexual chemistry with her GBF, who spends more time dressed as a laydee than David Walliams does. You do have to be very clear about where you stand with your S&MBF, and there can be no flirtatious frissons going on. My S&MBF and I do not fancy each other, but we do love each other like siblings, and he is invaluable in giving good advice from the alien perspective of the straight male (although several gay men I know have hoped to persuade him off his rampantly heterosexual path).

The SG knows how to have a seriously good time, and there are two types of playmates who particularly contribute to this. Girl Playmates are friends who you would not confide everything in, but are priceless at partying. Because you do not know them that well, you can neither strop nor be sombre in their company and thus they inevitably make you forget your cares and stay out for that just half a drink more...

There is another type of playmate who is just as vital – the Platonic Boyfriend, a male friend who you do not kiss but have minor sexual tension with, and who is liable to drift away if you get embroiled in a real relationship. I love Platonic Boyfriends. They are very useful as they will do DIY and run round after you in a way they never would if you slept with them; one of mine conveniently has offices ninety seconds from my flat so can be called on at a moment's notice to change light bulbs I cannot reach. He has also visited at 3 a.m. to locate my stopcock for me, without any indecent reference to his anatomy. Platonic Boyfriends can be the best company – you make each other look good; a proper male/female friendship always intrigues outsiders. I was once en route to the theatre with one whose supreme sexual reputation precedes him, and we contrived to lose the tickets – inside the Cabbage. Cue switching on the light, and scrabbling on all fours to locate them when we stopped at some traffic lights. On coming up for air, we realised we were outside the office of the man who broke my heart, and he happened to be leaving at the time so saw us. Whatever he assumed, his thunderous face suggested it was displeasing.

There are almost always moments with this type of friend when you are faced with the suggestion that you kiss, which we deal with later, because the moment any sort of bodily fluid is exchanged, he by very definition cannot be your Platonic Boyfriend any more. (None has, or ever will be, exchanged with Cabbage boy, but rumours circulate which we deny, or decline to put right, depending on how it suits us.)

To conclude the SG's balanced friendship circle, it is also useful to have a variety of blessing-counter friends who, along with being the stars that they are, make you realise how lucky you are. The first one being someone who is attached to a dreadful boyfriend/husband to make you thank God you are single. You have probably already got several; they are the type who own a lawnmower, and make you realise that if you have to settle for someone so dull as their other half you would rather get thee to a nunnery. There is also a good case for having an older/uglier friend to sympathise with about misbehaving work colleagues, parents and men. Slightly callous, perhaps, but admit it – you have some who fit the bill amongst your circle. Anyway, you are balanced because you also have a friend who is more beautiful than you, with whom you can sympathise about misbehaving work colleagues, parents and men. You may think the grass is greener for a supermodel type, but it is consoling to know that it is not. The most stunning woman I know is always having the most appalling time with the men in her world. Her most recent rake decided to embark on an affair – with her much younger half-sister. Her perfectly measured and reasonable response involved said lecher, some lube and YouTube.

Naturally, the final friend that every SG needs, and is almost beyond any other in importance, is a Bunbury. Bunbury, as mentioned before, is an Oscar Wilde creation from *The Importance of Being Earnest* – an imaginary friend who can provide a convenient excuse about or example for almost anything.

Finding Friends

Friends are fabulous, and it is always good to meet new ones. The trickiest times are when you move to somewhere new and your whole support network is suddenly miles away and you have to create a new one. I was living in New York in my early twenties and called up my father in tears, suffering homesickness from hell. He sagely pointed out that New York can be the most fantastic place in the world, but it can also be the loneliest. I figured out my way round it, obeying an all-knowing SG friend's mantra to 'never refuse an invitation'.

I am painfully shy, but have learnt to hide it well. Happiness will never be yours if you spend your whole time hiding under the duvet; you have to put yourself in harm's way to find it. If you are moving somewhere new, ask the friends you have if they know anyone you can connect with there and then be ruthless about getting out and meeting them. If this method is not supplying enough potential pals, take something up, whether it is skydiving or salsa. Stay sceptical and safe in regards to the Internet – one somewhat spaced out SG friend was shocked when she met up with a MySpace message man for munchies and found he was not quite the Matthew McConaughey lookalike his profile picture implied he was. (She is a proponent of the policy that you never know where a new friendship might lead, so aims to keep her latest acquaintances attractive...). Fortunately she had taken, on her Genuine Girlfriends' insistence, a karate-kicking friend as backup. After all, you never know – I once had a romantic interlude with a man I met online (although I did first Google image search him and check with mutual friends that he met my minimum height requirement of six foot before I agreed to meet him in the flesh).

If you find a new friend via an old one, you have to be careful not to put the introducer's nose out of joint by 'friend stealing'. Subsequent meet-ups, for a time, must always occur with the introducer present

– life is too short to make enemies because they have taken offence at your behaviour. I met my GBF via someone we now no longer see, and we were careful to let our relationship develop in her full knowledge and view before quietly losing touch with her. She spent so much time on her crackberry anyway that she deserved her gooseberry status.

However, this code of courtesy does not apply if you have met new friends through an ex. One SG friend met a fabulously fun set of playmates because of a boy she briefly dated. The wifebeater-wearing DJ (he took walking cliché to a new level) assumed she would be easily dispensable if things went awry, but what he had not counted on was that she would get on so well with everyone he knew. She went with it – his good-time inducing friends are compensation for his very short shortcomings. Her revenge on Mr Wifebeater was gratifyingly achieved every time she was guest-listed to yet another wild club night by his promoter pal, and to top it all off she even met her next love interest in front of her ex's decks in 'Ibeefa'.

Keeping Friends

Anything worthwhile – your body, your home, your work, your parents – requires maintenance, and your friends are no different. However, your friends should require nurture of the sort you wish to give, and if they do nothing but drain you, then you need to reassess. If someone is complaining that you have not called him or her, that may be true – but have they called you? Friendship goes both ways, it is about give and take. My friends and I contact each other, that is the deal; if neither party does, then perhaps it is not a friendship worth keeping, and you are both moving on.

You are a crazy-busy SG being pulled (and occasionally pulling) in different directions. That does not mean you need neglect your nearest and dearest. It is not always about physically seeing someone, it is just about contact, and for that the modern world with its plethora of communication tools is also your friend. It is so easy to make a quick call whilst tottering between appointments, or to send a one sentence e-mail or one-word text. (However, a word of warning: do try to remember to look as you cross roads. I have only ever been hit once, by a bicycle in front of a braying crowd outside the gay bar I was heading to. My reaction was slowed by four-inch heels – I was dressed for a Kylie lookalike contest at the time. Sadly my GBF's boyfriend beat me in the 'best hot pants' contest – it is so unfair how men get less cellulite than girls, however toxed they are.)

To me, friendship is about stopping and thinking about how the other person feels, and acting accordingly. I believe in real post; I never send a long missive, but real bits of paper that involve a stamp, whether it be a birthday or 'men are mean' card. When a girlfriend (or GBF) needs some TLC, these say so much more than an e-mail or text.

As part of being a friend, you should arrange rendezvouses, whether they be drinks, dinners, cinema or even holidays – often enough the things you do on a date, it is just you do not have to stress about the spot that appeared on your nose that morning. However, the onus must not be on you to organise everything; other people should too. I used to run myself ragged arranging reunions for all my schoolfriends thinking everything would fall apart if I was not on the case. Eventually I was so busy I had to let the others do it and, lo and behold, we all managed to meet up anyway – just in locations I would not have chosen. So I found the time to organise things again, and quit complaining!

In every friendship there will be awkward moments – it is a relationship after all, and people are tricky. You may have foibles that get on another's nerves. For instance, some like to divide a restaurant bill exactly, getting a calculator out, infuriating the more easy-going attendees. With such irritations all you can do is attempt not to resort to any playground-type behaviour. There are more serious occasions when measured confrontation may be called for, a typical time being if you gain a new friend. New friends can unsettle old friends, but we all need fresh blood and if they are feeling insecure, remind them they have a history with you that is irreplaceable; if they complain more, then they are being irrational. You need to be honest and tell them so.

Wingman Selection

The term 'Wingman' is no longer the exclusive domain of pitiable males working in tandem on the pull, where they spy two females and one takes the 'uglier' one out of the equation by chatting her up whilst leaving his friend to go in for the kill with the other. The designation has, quite rightly and only naturally, been appropriated by the SG and now 'Wingman' is another expression to add to the older one of 'Walker', used to describe the person from among your friends whom you choose to accompany you to events/nights out etc. It is rare that you won't be allowed a 'plus one', and if you are not, it suggests a set-up by whoever is hosting – odd numbers upset vibes and placements. It is no mean feat to select the right Wingman for the right occasion. It could be your GBF, a Genuine Girlfriend, or one of your selection of Platonic Boyfriends (although there is the danger of getting drunk and sleeping with them, see Accidental Sex in Chapter Eight).

The Wingman is the essential accessory to every outfit. You need to avoid picking someone who is going to be a Social Hand Grenade and embarrass you in some way, or who will be ill at ease and unable to cope with the event – it is unfair on them and you. For theatre things I always take my S&MBF who works the room like a smouldering knife through butter when we lose each other, especially if there are tall, tricky actresses present. Once when he was unavailable I made the mistake of taking one of my other Platonic Boyfriends and he was like a fish out of water. It was a disservice that I will not be repeating; his handsome self was too overwhelmed by a deluge of West End Wendys. By the same token, I completely accept that I will not be the person my friends go to if they want to take a camping holiday – I will not be an asset; I like my running water to involve a tap. Think carefully about who is going to be there, how much time you can spend with the person you are taking and whether they will manage or malfunction if you have to leave them on their own for a while. They should also have the capacity to **pull the ripcord** for you and get a somewhat tired and emotional you out of an event and safely home (accidents occasionally do happen, and the danger exists that you may sometimes prop up a bar a little too long).

In my experience, gay friends tend to make the best wingmen; almost everyone thinks they are entertaining and there is never the awkward possibility they will get amorous in your direction and you will have to fend off a lunge at the end of the evening. Chivalry is not dead – it is just vanquished to the realm of the gay man. The ones I know are far more gallant than any of my straight male friends, who if they offer to walk you home, only bother in the hope of a kiss, whilst the former always do so just because it is the right thing to do.

Impossible Friends

Friends should be the one area of life which is almost always plain sailing, otherwise why have you let them into your world? Sometimes, however, it is only inevitable there will be some rocking of the boat.

Everyone has rough patches, and it is essential that you be there for a friend in need if they are going through one, but you cannot also be their therapist. One girlfriend seems to collect depressives. Something in her obviously likes the feeling of being needed, but at the same time they have all expected so much from her that she has ended up seeing a counsellor herself. Friends have to acknowledge that they need to help themselves; if they really are in that bad a state, they must go to the professionals and if necessary, resort to Prozac.

You are not a fair-weather friend. But there has to be balance for a friendship to work. If someone is just draining you when you have nothing left to give, then there will come a point where you have to be cruel to be kind, and either not see them for a bit or tell them what they are doing to you and that they need help you cannot bestow. If neither somewhat crushingly candid approach appeals, try the classic Bunbury tactic, claiming that she is at her wit's end about a perplexing pal and is about to tell her they need professional help/to get a life, or indeed just claim that it is Bunbury who is causing you the trouble.

There are friends who are bad for you for different reasons. I am in recovery from a thyroid problem. I like alcohol, but I should not drink it to excess; some friends support me, and raise their eyebrows the minute I look inclined towards polishing off the bottle, whilst others surreptitiously fill up my glass. There are also friends who are great for some things, such as dancing until dawn, but not others – illegal substances have never been my thing. Sometimes friends do not want to hang out with me if the evening degenerates in this direction because they think I am boring, but by the same token, I am always happy to leave at that point. When they hoover cocaine, people are like hurricanes leaving a path of destruction in their wake. This is always beyond tedious for those who are not high, and whom it invariably falls upon to amend the immediate devastation, all the more so since the cokeheads concerned are under the chemical misapprehension that they are being the life and soul.

It is only natural that as we age, we sometimes drift apart. I happen to still be incredibly close to a few schoolfriends, but fewer university friends. It is not that they are not lovely, but they have nothing in common with me, the SG, when they are married and not going out every night for work or play but are safely ensconced in their significantly square-footaged houses. Our compatibility has simply changed as our priorities have. The difficulty with drifting apart is when you are the first person to realise that you have both outgrown the friendship. My thirtieth birthday dinner is proving a minefield to negotiate. I realise that several people's noses will be out of joint if they are not invited, despite the fact that some have no idea of my e-mail address, even though I have had it for over two years. The owners of the disjointed noses are all in couples who also cannot comprehend why I would possibly NFI their partner, although I have only met them twice, nor why I complain that my mobile's SIM card is too small for the catalogue of numbers I need. It is partly because I am out every night and I like collecting people, but it is also because I do not cook, so I have a lot of takeaways in my phone's address book, whilst these couples seem to mostly stay in, utilising a strange tome called a recipe book. Indeed, I have a coupled-up friend of this type who hardly ever uses her mobile, whilst the bill for mine is my biggest expense after shoes.

These attached female types can get irritating, and thus the drift occurs. Pre-engagement, they are stressed about the possibility of a ring and so are always cancelling on you for him, after the wedding they often become boring, and in-between they become... Bridezilla. Bridezilla has no idea how uninteresting she is. The adornment on her wedding ring finger is distasteful, her ideas of a hen night hideous, and her giant doily of a wedding dress is almost as unsightly as the proposed flower arrangements she insists on discussing in great detail with you, even though your knowledge of flora only extends to identifying what colour it is. (Of course, your engaged friend may never turn into Bridezilla and be lovely throughout – I do know a few. But they are not in the majority.)

Try and put Bridezilla off from talking to you about the wedding topic by setting up a get-together with a mutual friend who has toddlers and does not get enough adult conversation and failing to appear. If she really insists on your involvement in the wedding preparations, you may have to tell a little white lie and make out that you dislike discussing nuptials because they make you feel so alone. An untruth, as her beloved bores for Britain and you would rather never sleep with anyone again than make a lifetime commitment to someone of his ilk, but it might shut her up.

The other area where friendships can be sorely tested is working with a pal – in some ways it is almost like kissing them and can prove the kiss of death to your camaraderie. I have twice made the mistake of getting involved with friends business-wise. The first arrangement dissolved amicably; we were both women, we both realised we could not give the other what they needed, and we talked it through, only bringing in the lawyers late in the day to resolve the issue officially. The second was tougher – a man felt I had done him ill, but two of his BFs and my lawyer both said he could not deliver and would let me down if I continued my association with him.

Occasionally, when a friend turns out to be a nightmare, it may become essential to drop them. If this is so, do just try and let the relationship run its course by straying out of touch rather than having a massive rift with each other. It is always possible to encourage this by not replying to texts or e-mails from them asking if this is still your mobile number or e-mail address...

Enemies

The old adage 'Keep your friends close, your enemies closer,' is a shrewd one. Estranging people is immensely dangerous – losing touch is one thing, but pissing someone off is something else entirely. Turn on the killer charm if necessary around people you distrust; you are smarter than they are. You do not want to give such types ammunition to besmirch your reputation – other people will always believe the bad stuff said about you first. One SG was driven to distraction by an attached acquaintance who thought she had been flirting with her husband (she hadn't) and who then went bad-mouthing her around town. Only by the SG saying lovely things to all and sundry about Mrs Nutcase for a lengthy period did it finally dawn on the world at large who in actuality deserved the b*tch reputation.

Then there are the people brought into your world because your friends are dating them. My girlfriends tend to bring in either bastards, who always give good conversation but who treat them dreadfully, or nice but dull men. Be pleasant, but there is no need to put yourself out for them if it is obvious they are going to last no longer than an iPod battery. My male friends tend to be more controversial in choice, as they are often thinking with their brains even less, and date women who give the fairer sex a bad name. There are countless examples – one playboy of a Platonic Boyfriend slept his way around London before the tables were eventually turned on him. It would have been amusing to see the player being played, except the girl in question was a gold-digger. She had no girlfriends – the worst sign – and had slept with most of his friends before casting her eye on him when she had cast-iron proof his was the biggest... bank balance. We made our feelings known to him, then took a step back and let her dig her own grave. Never force a besotted friend to choose between their lover and you, because the sex will always win through. Let them get out of the honeymoon period first.

There is another variety of unfortunate girl men seem to go for – the small, squeaky stupid ones. A **Squeaky** is a 'man's woman' rather than a woman's woman, the type who will ignore every girl present if there is a boy there for her to flirt with, and would certainly never abide by the girls' code, kissing any man if she thinks it might get her somewhere. They always giggle at appalling jokes if made by their target, flutter their overly mascara'd eyelashes, only eat half of what they are given, including things like Jelly Babies, and expect men to pay for it all because they have to spend money on essentials like shoes. Every girl needs shoes, but nice girls will never be out to bankrupt a boy. I know a lot of Squeakies, and one friend even ditched her then boyfriend partly because he insisted on hanging out with his best mate and his Squeaky girlfriend every weekend and both boys held her in high regard. To really irritate a Squeaky, monopolise her in an overtly lovely manner when she is in male company. She will be desperate to ditch you for more social mountaineering interaction, but she cannot be rude within a gentleman's earshot, and if she is, the little madam is shooting herself in her little tippy-toes. If you are stuck on your own, compliment her about her nail varnish/lipstick. She will go on forever about where she found them and you will have to think of nothing further to say to the airhead whilst you contemplate serious issues, such as who will win *Strictly Come Dancing*.

Of course, if your friends permanently attach themselves to these people, they have to be tolerated. Your opinion, if it is asked for, must be measured. If you are honest about your thoughts regarding their beloved and they marry, it is a disaster... but then again if they marry that may be a disaster in itself. With a divorce rate of almost one in two, for any couple of whatever income, but especially if there is not much in the bank to go round if it all goes t*ts up, a pre-nup is something as a friend you should be suggesting.

Whatever you do, it is best not done at the wedding, management of which – along with that of other events – we now survey.

Chapter Six

Event Management

Event management covers practically all excursions from outside a 50-metre radius of your home.

Being out is the oxygen, the very lifeblood, of the SG. We SGs are not tied to our abodes by any sort of strings, apron or otherwise, and thus have the opportunity to get out there and enjoy ourselves more and better than any of our contemporaries obliged to consider their 'better' half. However, because of our expertise in periods spent outside our households, we are inevitably more discerning about what fun is – we know the difference between having it large and having it very small indeed. It is not necessary for SGs to waste their time at a soirée they consider substandard when they can easily get to an alternative one, without accounting for a belligerent boyfriend enthralled by dull discussion and bad beer.

Remember, as with work events, you do not have to accept every invitation (you are a desired and desirable SG – if you attended every opening of an envelope you would be in danger of acquiring bags; and I am not talking about the Louis Vuitton variety). Bunbury has the convenient (for you, at least) tendency to have a breakdown and require your precious presence at the most select moments. Indeed, Bunbury's state of mind may be such that you will only know at the last minute, when your host has given you the exact details of the occasion, whether you will be able to leave their side, although naturally you may have to rush back to Bunbury at a beeping phone's notice (prime a friend to text/call you). However, in general, I am a great believer in attending something for a short while to discover if you are missing anything or not. As my grandmother says, you can sleep in your armchair when you're old.

Human beings are, by their very nature, contrary, thus if you are trapped and told to have a good time, it is highly likely you will not. It is therefore wise to avoid boat parties that actually involve any sailing, and foreign places where you are miles from the airport and unable to get transportation out. I once suffered a torturous evening with an ex-boyfriend on a boat cruising the Thames. He hid until the anchor raised, wise enough to realise I would have scarpered back down the gangplank if he had appeared before we had set off, and then ambushed me, determined to convince me he was a good catch despite his infidelity. Salt was rubbed into my wounds still further by the unobstructed view of empty Cabbages with yellow lights whipping down the Embankment.

This does not mean you should never attend soirées in obscure locations – they can be fun – it is just that you should always retain the ability to pull the ripcord if needs be. It should be possible to pre-book a Cabbage almost anywhere, and the more remote the venue the less such transport will be available and it is all the wiser to have one reserved under your name. You can invariably move the collection time to later or cancel it altogether if you are having a spectacular time. Knowing there is the option to leave somehow provides a sense of liberating freedom that allows an SG to revel ever more raucously. It also means your vibe at the end of the evening is not ruined by having to wend a ridiculous route home. My Wingman for a recent foray forgot to pre-book a Cabbage and so I had to walk home at midnight barefoot (the four-inch heels were just too much), behaviour not clever enough at the best of times, but especially through Soho in the bleak mid-winter.

Along with establishing your exit strategy, much of your delectation of the gathering will stem from how you have managed your expectations prior to it – some of the fun of the fair is in the anticipation, but too high and the event could be a real let-down. Experience dictates that the occasions you expect to be fabulous will habitually not live up to the prospect, whilst those you are somewhat dreading are the most fun. It is why school nights (Sunday to Wednesday – Thursday does not count as a weekday because you only have one day of work to get through) are so often the best evenings out: unlike weekend evenings, there is less build-up, so you can be surprised into having a good time. The minute you have banked on having a Sunday morning hangover it will probably not be that acute, whilst if you are confirmed for a 7 a.m. Tuesday step class the sum total of your activity will be hitting your alarm's snooze button. Surprise can lead to such satisfaction.

Once all this is taken into account, you must concentrate on you. To sparkle you have to feel good about yourself, so get to grips with your body beautiful and pull yourself together into a package that will shine, but still be suitable for the event. Your outfit for the sweatiness of the Space club in Ibiza will not be the same as for your sister's wedding, so think hard as to whether Skechers or stilettos are the more seemly. The aim is to wear something that fits the occasion, but that maintains your individuality. Heaven forbid you should blend in; you are in your prime – this is not the period of your life to be a wallflower.

Next, after selecting your most becoming Wingman (assuming you are not required to attend alone), set about composing your CL. It will depend on the event in question as to how much research is necessary, indeed possible. The first thing to try to find out is who else is going to be there. If you have not been privy to the guest list, a moment of thought will probably allow you to construct it anyway, at least partially – from the tricky relative to the work colleague the host or hostess owes an invite. I have done this ever since I entered into a diatribe before dinner insulting a recently released film... only to discover that the person I was being vile about it to had designed the sets for it. He took mass offence, and the dinner was a disaster. Oops. After a period where she would NFI me, the hostess concerned has begun to include me on her invite list again – but always calls me up to FYI me on guests first.

If you suspect conversation could get sticky, bring a prop. I have a handbag with the Maltesers logo beaded on it, into which I insert real packets of Maltesers (my Wingman has to carry my wallet and keys as this modus operandi doesn't leave any room for inedible items). My doling out of lighter-than-ordinary-chocolate always goes down a veritable exclamation-producing storm.

Although each host would like to think that their event is unique, there are some standard occasions that require their own SG brand of management.

The Drinks Party

The most regular affair in your SG diary will be The Drinks Party. This can range on the glamour scale from a house party at a friend's with a pile of six-packs and several trips to the offie, to a cocktail party where the champagne just will not run out, however hard you all try. The challenges for the SG are the same whatever the venue. You need to take charge to make sure you get through the evening without serious incident, ensuring you are sober enough to get yourself home safely afterwards – Weetabix before you head out to play always helps.

On making your entrance, do a circuit of the venue noting bathroom facilities and likely waiting times, and then position yourself by the kitchen. If at a posh party, this means you will be first in line for the canapés and may actually manage to line your tummy slightly more – eating is not cheating, despite whatever mantra the size zero brigade abide by. Being by the kitchen also gives you the added bonus of meeting fun people who are doing the same thing, as they will be of similar outlook to you – experienced party goers and often single. Indeed, one of my boyfriends came into my world because he had had the same bright idea and we bonded over miniature Yorkshire puddings. By the same token, kitchens are always the most packed places at house parties and their slightly brighter lighting will put off spotty Simon from thinking he can lunge at you, whilst you can concentrate your attentions on studying more agreeable specimens.

You are a fabulously well turned out SG, you are sociable and know a lot of people, and at these occasions souls who do not get out as much and have as many people to remember will inevitably recognise and greet you by name, when you cannot recall theirs. It is always possible to brazen it out with exclamations of 'Where have you been?' or 'When did we last see each other?'. This works well, until you then have to introduce them to someone else. However, there is a tactic to help spare your blushes here. Gesticulate between the two saying 'Have you met?', and proceed to take an elaborate sip of your beverage. They should then take the bait and introduce themselves to each other.

Do not panic if you turn up in an identical outfit to another girl, even if they are four sizes smaller than you. Laugh good-naturedly, compliment her on the one thing she has done differently, such as her lipstick shade (focusing on a part of any girl's outfit in a flattering fashion is always a reliable bonding tool), and if her hackles were rising they will be smoothed back down in no time.

You may encounter people with whom you do not wish to exchange more than minimum pleasantries. Always prime your Wingman to a subtle signal – gently placing your hand on your throat for instance –

which you will employ if you need rescuing from someone dreadful. Also have another movement for the reverse – indicating that you wish to be left alone with the person you are talking to, as they are particularly fascinating in some way, whether it be the banter or the brown eyes. Your Wingman will be able to cope without you; you will have picked one who can.

The Couply Dinner Party

The next obstacle course of an event the SG has to contend with is the Couply Dinner Party, held by a pair of your very married or attached friends who have a kitchen cupboard containing ramekins and springform cake tins. Beware that it could be a set-up with a bachelor of some description, indicated by their refusal to allow you to take a Wingman and everyone else but he bringing a long-term partner. These friends' ministrations throughout the episode will be about as understated as an Ugg boot and they are unlikely to hit the nail on the head with their nominee. The proposed new man will probably have intolerable prejudices or just be looking for his first post-separation fling before he goes back to his wife and small children.

Although your initial instinct may be to decline the couply dinner party, pause and reflect before you do. Improbable though it is, you may have an interesting evening (I picked up one of my gay wingmen from one). Arrive fifteen minutes after you were asked to, so as to allow awkward children and other halves to be settled, and bring something you want to eat or drink. If they are the type who have everything, just bring your hostess a candle from a shop that has a classy carrier bag. It is always about where the present was ostensibly sourced, never mind how the candle smells or where it was actually from, as they will never light it and will probably palm it off on someone else anyway.

Take control and implement your CL early on, bracing yourself for the inevitable SG third degree. The attached's first query will not be about your health, spectacular shoes or flattering make-up, nor even your recent promotion. It will be about your love life. This is partly so the attached inquisitor can be smug, partly so they can live vicariously through you. Make sure by the time you are done with them, detailing your fun work, holidays and naughty playtime, that all self-satisfied smirks have been wiped from the sceptic's face. You are open to meeting people, but at the same time you are not about to settle for substandard options. Do not feel you have to defend your choices – you are who you are, at peace with yourself. That will shine through, and if they do not recognise what is self-evident, it is their problem and leave them to discuss garden sheds and DIY with someone who cares.

Whilst you are regaling a rapt table in best SG superb-value-style with an amusing anecdote, a Joiner may reveal themselves. Not content with causing professional headaches to the SG, Joiners are never off duty, as they like their waking hours to be worthy. These orthodox souls – often in religion as well as outlook – will either interject with a comment about your dubious morals (as in, you may have slept with more than one person), or come up with an inappropriate suggestion along the lines of: 'Have you thought about the Alpha course for meeting someone? That's where I met my [smug look] other half.' One girlfriend of mine confronted by such sanctimonious behaviour was able to come back with the memorable – and true – riposte, 'No, I'm Jewish.' Joiners do not have the manners or the self-censorship button required to know that you do not bring religion or politics up unless you are bored and want to destroy an evening.

Always help the host or hostess clear the tables – if you have a nightmare draw on the table-seating front it means you have a break from talking to your tedious neighbour, and it can also allow you to surreptitiously slip off to adjust your leaving strategy on your always handy (although subtly secreted and if possible on 'silent' mode) mobile if required. It is also polite, of course. This, along with trips to the loo (although never too many so you are forced to refute rumours that you are **doing dinner off the mirror** – i.e. hoovering cocaine – and/or battling bulimia), can provide a much needed respite, allowing you to collect yourself to maintain your SG brand of bubbliness.

The School/University Reunion

Another event that can bring unnecessary pressure to the SG for all sorts of reasons is the school or university reunion. The worst traits in people often expose themselves at these gatherings, as they seek to justify their existence over the past decade or so to their peers. If you accept the invite to go, you must be aware that some who attend will decide your SG status is an Achilles heel on which they will focus to deflect from their own shortcomings, rather than the positive achievement you have made it. That said, reunions can prove worthwhile, with old friends coming back into your world.

At a reunion you can either opt to rise above any bad behaviour from others and just be your usual incredible self, or get subversive. I would like to say I always choose the former path, but it tends to be the latter as these occasions bring out my more mischievous side. I have not yet stooped to the level of a male friend, who hired some bling and a blonde for one university event – something that he has repented of at length because the college's development office are now always begging him for cash. However, I tend to push the boundaries of appropriate dress, wearing an outfit that shows off to maximum effect a body that is most definitely pre-baby and certainly not matching the calorie consumption of a podgy partner.

There are always various beings taking the whole thing too seriously, or under the misapprehension they are having fun as the last time they went out properly was the school disco in 1991. You may well look at your watch thinking it is time to leave when only ten minutes have elapsed since your arrival. However, revel in the reinforced truth that you are happy and running above the rat race that so many of your contemporaries think is so important but is actually so destructive to their well-being. You can then go on to enjoy some time with your friends who have a life.

The Engagement Party

By the very nature of being an SG, even if you are not finding another's impending matrimony bitter-sweet, some people will be looking at you with a mix of pity and superiority as though you are. As though to prolong this patronising assault, and in direct proportion to the shrinking length of time that modern day matrimonial vows last, happy couples seem increasingly to feel the need to stretch out their nuptials. If you are really unlucky, those involved will have come over all American and will hold endless pre- and post-wedding affairs on top of the big day itself. You may find you have no choice but to turn up to them all, no rescuing by Bunbury allowed for an occasion so significant.

At the minimum you will start off having to cope with the engagement party, where even the nicest attached people can just be irritatingly smug. Try to limit your time at it and have a Wingman with a similar state of mind to yours. On arrival, you will no doubt feel obliged to offer a hearty 'Congratulations'. If you are unsure about the union and cannot quite bring yourself to utter this, follow my GBF's tactic of expressing a supremely sincere 'Well done'. Well done for a good match? For achieving their five-year plan box-ticking goals? For what, exactly? It really is a delightfully Machiavellian phrase, so utterly ambiguous. However, if this is an occasion where you will be utilising it, perhaps plan to leave before you have had one too many cocktails – you do not want to jeopardise your self-censorship faculty.

The Hen Night

Unfortunately your status of SG means that you will probably not be able to avoid being dragged into arrangements over the hen night; because you are someone who still goes out, you will probably be one of the few people Bridezilla knows who is capable of organising it.

Brides are strange souls; perfectly normal people who will suddenly decide they need to have pole-dancing lessons to say goodbye to the 'single' life when they have not been near it in years. The one rule about hen nights is to assume they are going to be dire; manage your expectations early on. Like Christmas, they are designed for people who do not have much of a life, and if they degenerate into any form of wild occasion, it is only because it is the first time in months the guests have got out of the house. However, at the stroke of midnight there will invariably be an exodus as various attendees, like aged Cinderellas but with shabby shoes, dash home to relieve the babysitter. Naturally, Prince Charming is not at home to look after the baby this one time he's granted his Cinders a 'pink ticket' as he will have to be out on his regular pub night.

Now indulge me a momentary lapse into cynicism, SG prerogative if you will, but the trend for going away for hen weekends is ridiculous – weddings are expensive enough to attend. You are perfectly within your rights to refuse to make one in Magaluf on the basis you have to go do something essential with Bunbury (who has also got me out of canoeing).

If, as is likely, you are landed with organising the hen party, you will be expected to anticipate the bride's wishes. In attitude she will be becoming relative-like with a touch of diva thrown in, and instead of being specific, spelling out what she wants in the usual friend-like honest manner, will think it more tactful to hint. This is a nightmare, because whatever you do, you will get the tone wrong. One bride-to-be I know was most emphatic that she did not want to have a fake veil or any such paraphernalia, but was then devastated she did not have a prop to distinguish her from the rest of the party. Make it very clear at the beginning that the bridal brat has to be transparent in her briefing, and that she must not expect you to be a mind-reader.

The Wedding

Thereby follows the wedding. Your attendance will be compulsory unless the happy couple are not close friends or relatives; or you are a minor celebrity, have spied an *OK!* magazine logo on the invite and have somewhere better to sell your soul that day.

There are two distinct schools of thought about being a member of a bridal party, and you will probably have entrenched views either way. For some SGs, if the bride is lovely, then being primped and preened and wearing a tailor-made frock will be a joyful experience. However, others, including myself, fall firmly in the other camp, believing that being a big (as in aged in double figures) bridesmaid is nothing short of hideous humiliation that family and even friends may try to heap on the SG, thinking for some reason you are lonely and will wish to get involved to keep busy. The bride is unlikely to want you to look better than them so will invariably dress you in bronze. Added to which, what assortment of twenty-/thirty-something women have figures that all look good in the same style dress? They do not. If you want to be a bridesmaid, think long and hard about who is at the helm, and if she is liable to manifest any Bridezilla tendencies, proceed at your peril. You will have to deal with her tantrums (almost matched by those of small people in absurd outfits in the same shade as yours), mothers at war, drunken ushers leering – it goes on. It can be perfectly sensible to turn bridesmaidship down and give yourself a chance of delighting in the wedding breakfast. If your maximum enjoyment of the woman in white's day will only come if you can hide on the back pew with your Platonic Boyfriends and giggle, before having the freedom to flit about the reception as you please with no mother-of-the-bride attending responsibilities, try and do everything you can to get out of being on the front line with Bridezilla. Your enthusiastic look at the nuptials might then even be genuine for the first hour of the eight-hour marathon that these things always end up being.

If you are fortunate you will have known the person asking you to parade in taffeta for years, and are therefore able to lay the groundwork for refusing voluminous-dress-wearing duties early, even before they have met 'the one'. When a university friend got married, she was not at all offended when she asked and I refused to be her bridesmaid – I had spent almost ten years banging on about how big bridesmaids are a bad idea. It is not so easy if a new bride marrying into the family has asked you for politeness' sake. If this is the case, gently explain that being a big bridesmaid is just not you, but suggest a person whose age matches your shoe size, and who would love the chance to wear a frilly dress. You could also offer to do a reading or some other job that involves next to no work. If she complains, fake a minor breakdown bemoaning your singledom, claiming being a bridesmaid just makes you feel you would be living up to the adage, 'always a bridesmaid, never a bride' and you just cannot take it. Once you have sent her off home to her dull other half and pre-wedding diet you can then totter off to have a calorific cocktail with your S&MBF.

As an SG you want to try and elicit maximum brownie points from the happy couple before the wedding to increase your chances of a good draw at the meal after. Buy them a present from the wedding list – they really do not want you to go off message and get unique on them, they want enough people to contribute so they have a dinner service. Do it early – in these initial stages they will be logging onto John Lewis online every day to see who has bought what from their list, whilst by the end of the run the thrill will have gone and the chance to get to the top of their good books will be wasted. You will also then manage to buy a half-decent present rather than bathroom fittings or, even worse, bed linen, which I have never understood why brides-to-be think should be aired in public in such a way.

When you have absconded from as many obligations as possible, the final stage in the preparations is to put together your flattering outfit. An ex-boyfriend's wedding is immediate authorisation for you to max your credit card out as it is vital you look simply (just not too stridently sexily) stunning, and any bank manager will understand that. Hopefully you will be allowed a Wingman for this one, but if not, and you think it may be too hard, do not go. I have been to an ex-boyfriend's wedding and it was wonderful closure, I made my peace with him and my past whilst having a ball with several Platonic Boyfriends. Another SG ex of his, who sat in the pew in front of me, found it harder, and was in floods of tears. Unless you were jilted by Prince William, such histrionics really aren't called for, although it is always easier to move on if you are wearing particularly beautiful footwear.

Deducing the likely attendees will also assist you in pitching your expectations for the event and mean you are less put out when you are sat next to dear deaf Uncle David as you are the only person he has anything to say to, even if it is only ever 'What?'

Your Wingman, thanks to number capping, may be restricted to someone already on the guest list and not be a close friend. However, as a single soul it is useful to have one just to cut the significant costs that these events entail – from sharing petrol bills to a room at the dubious local hotel listed on the carefully worded 'fact sheet' you were sent and then lost with the invite. However, make clear the ground rules – a friend of mine split the cost of a room with a girl she hardly knew, who scandalously pulled the groom's (divorced) dad, and my friend was left without a bed for the night. If possible, I will always pre-order a car home if it is within a thirty-mile radius of my door as it costs the same as a B&B/hotel and means I will wake up in my own bed and still have some weekend to play in as I see fit. If I want to after-party there is typically someone crazy enough to offer their room (and room service) for abuse, and the taxi can be put off until I am done playing there.

Try to keep your behaviour almost solemn during the service itself, although some are unintentionally hilarious. Research beforehand what type of ceremony it is – i.e. how long it is going to be. I have done from ten minutes to two hours, the latter being for a 'happy-clappy' wedding where they got the synthesisers, drums and microphones out and the laughter got infectious at the back of the church.

At the reception, the imbibe-alcohol-early mantra is a good tactic to follow. Not only will this anaesthetise you to the effects of the people at your table asking why you are an SG, but also the booze at the beginning of the wedding is always going to be superior to the dregs at the end, which you may well have to pay for. However, please remember to sober up during the meal; losing control of bodily functions, which I have witnessed SGs do at a wedding, is just not a good look, especially if you have been forced to fly solo – who is going to look after you? It will also contribute to any 'poor her' whisperings. If you can, check the table plan early on at the reception to establish your whereabouts so you do not exhaust your conversation with anyone on your table before you even get there. It is exceptionally bad form to change the name cards on the table to improve your draw, however tempting it may be – Bridezilla will have spent months on the seating plan and it will be noted. I spied an SG relation of mine doing it once, and while they were not looking, I changed it back. They had a surprisingly good time, much more so than if they had sat next to the safe bet they selected, as well as not treading on the bride's toes.

The aim of your CL will be to keep all discussion frothy – this is not the moment to launch into deep and meaningful discussions of any description. There will be a certain quota of the attendees who will focus on your alleged need to catch the bridal bouquet, so before they launch into the topic, divert with talk of the beautiful flower arrangements. Early on in proceedings find a non-controversial detail – the bride's dress buttons, the sermon, the mother-of-the-bride's splendid hat, the sweepstake on how long the speeches are going to last – and wax lyrical about these throughout the day. You can even carry it on into the thank you letter, which you must send promptly to whoever mortgaged themselves to the eyeballs to pay for the lukewarm champagne and rubbery salmon.

There will probably be moments at a wedding where you will feel very single and a little wistful, especially if it is a younger sibling who is tying the knot. Keep it in perspective. Focus on the *Groundhog Day* elements of the occasion – the conversation, the bickering relatives, the tasteless food – and this will hopefully allow you an air of amused detachment for most of the proceedings. And if you need to get Eeyore about it, you are allowed to remind yourself about modern day divorce rates.

The one good thing about a person's wedding is that it should be a one-off (with second ones Bunbury is allowed and you can turn down the invites), and although there are often stages of the year where there is a glut, they are just phases. Not so with New Year's Eve, which seems to come around quicker with each passing year and is usually an overpriced, depressing, waste of time.

New Year's Eve

There are two ways for the SG to play the launch of the most depressing month of the year. (I will not accept any arguments to the contrary – the weather in January is foul, it is dark, and no one has any money as they were paid early in December, blew it all over Christmas, and it is a long month.) Dismiss out of hand the pressure to find someone to kiss (just think, if you do not, you are probably less likely to get ill – there are a lot of germs floating around at that time of year). Invariably the best New Year's Eves are where you almost forget to 'celebrate' midnight – because you were enjoying yourself too much, i.e. you had forgotten about why you were there. Thus either be aggressively organised and do something you were planning to do anyway – visit Edinburgh, have a house-warming party, fork out a month's salary at a posh restaurant – or leave it to the very last minute and go with the flow. My best New Year's Eve was planned on the day itself, when two Genuine Girlfriends came to mine for a sleepover, we drank champagne, ate yummy nibbles and watched trashy teen movies. We were too busy ogling Keanu Reeves to switch the television over to watch Big Ben, then had a relatively early night and woke up the next day hangover-free with wallets intact.

Birthday SG

The other event that will come along with increasingly rapid regularity is your birthday. You are probably in the position where you have realised that your birthday does not belong to you; it belongs to other people, and as an SG you will have an awful lot in your world wanting a piece of you. As a result, it can be a painstaking process to get right – everything will require more attention than you have time for, from guest list to venue to budget. However, going Big Duvet in an attempt to pretend it is not happening is not allowed as your friends will want to celebrate you; only scheduling an operation has got me out of having to plan something. If you do not want to resort to hospitalising yourself, I suggest going for a low-key pub night. Make sure your Genuine Girlfriends are coming, tell everyone where you will be, and expect nothing. You will not be disappointed by flakes, and may even end up having the time of your life when hundreds of people descend and you dance until dawn.

Fabulous Footloose SG

For there is nothing like the spur of the moment. In this chapter I am not for one minute advocating that you should plan your life so much you have no room for spontaneity, which is what being single should be all about. You can just leave the house without notifying anyone – Bunbury, escape routes and CLs are just ways of trying to ensure you have a good time. The mobile phone exists for you to always be in touch with friends in other locations who can advise you to turn up or stay away as their party is either getting started or ending. 'Stay in Radio Contact' is the mantra I so often cry to those I know out and about and on the town. I regularly send spies somewhere first, and if the event is any good they text me – nine times out of ten I slap some lip gloss on and go and join them. Better miss sleep than miss out.

My grandmother should be proud (although I'm sure she would like me to learn how to use my oven too).

The more you are out, the more you will be out; there will be a domino effect in invites. The preparation you do, from the CL to the fun Wingman you bring, means that people will want to be around you. On some nights you may even find yourself double, perhaps even triple parking, social engagements, flitting from occasion to occasion in beautiful butterfly manner. However, sometimes you will find yourself NFI'd to an event you wish to attend.

NFI

Being NFI'd is not necessarily something you should take abjectly to heart, but it is worth briefly contemplating why you were. When you put yourself in the host's or hostess's shoes there is probably a myriad of acceptable reasons: there may be a guest you do not gel with attending, numbers are particularly tight – or it could be that they just forgot to invite you. Kicking up an obvious fuss is only going to incline people to NFI you more, so do not, unless it is in a light-hearted, obviously teasing, manner that leaves no room for misinterpretation.

If there is absolutely no good reason why they should not squeeze a fabulous SG in, there are ways of getting your way, although use the tactics sparingly, since if you irritate anyone in the process you will soon enough find yourself justifiably NFI'd in the future. One SG I know, who admittedly possesses a touch of the social mountaineer about her, was NFI'd to a particularly high-powered dinner party. She called the hostess up and invited her for dinner *à deux* at a restaurant on the same night. The mountaineer knew full well the hostess would say that she could not attend because she had a dinner, which out of politeness the mountaineer would be invited to join instead. The principle works for most events, pub or party.

The other main reason you may find yourself NFI'd is the spectre of the ex. The host could be better friends with him, and feel that your being in the same room will create awkwardness. If this drives you crazy, since the last thing you want is such a creature seriously impacting on your social life, you will need to take a deep breath and come to terms with their existence and their behaviour, both past and present. Always maintain a dignified composure in his presence even if you're crying inside, so that everyone in the vicinity can see that you are fine and you are not going to ruin the vibe of an evening by turning on the waterworks. Two members of my circle of friends went out with each other for years, and then he broke up with her because of 'work pressures'. This over-used excuse was proven hollow when he, in a particularly male manner, moved on within a fortnight, right in front of my now SG friend's nose. She was just leaving a nightclub at 3 a.m. and he pushed past her in the taxi queue bundling a woman into a cab, loudly announcing his address. She went home, cried for 24 hours, and had to make the decision. She still wanted to see their mutual friends, not all would sacrifice him for her, and therefore she needed to be a grown-up about it. She rose above it all, made sure she was seen out there having fun in the presence of him and his new girlfriend, only ever breaking down in private onto the shoulder of her Genuine Girlfriends. The new woman in his life quickly revealed herself as a prize b*tch, all his friends loathed her, she got dumped and he now quizzes the SG about any of her love prospects, which are always far superior to his own. Even more pleasing, they are better friends than before they dated and he now buys her drinks when they are out playing instead of making her the designated driver.

Carriages

Always send a thank you note of some description, or even a present, to any event host or hostess. You could even stock up a 'present drawer' full of useless gifts you have received that you can palm off on others; however, make sure you keep track of things. I was once given a box of chocolates from a friend as a thank you which I had given her a year before. It was definitely the same one; the shop assistant had accidentally put a marker pen against the label, and they were also by this stage past their use-by date. Smirnoff the cat enjoyed munching them, although they did make him even more schizophrenic than usual.

With these small steps, events should prove to be an enjoyable time rather than endurance tests. And, it is whilst out living and loving life that you will inevitably come across a new Distraction of the male variety. When you least expect it, potential Objects tend to appear, demanding your details. For when bosses, parents, friends and room-mates are being successfully managed, you are happy, and that turns the male species into a giddy moth to your contentedly flickering flame. In best SG style you must be prepared, from keeping business cards on your person to learning how to text away, to assist these Objects in causing your phone to make noises, and to such Distractions and tools we now turn.

Chapter Seven

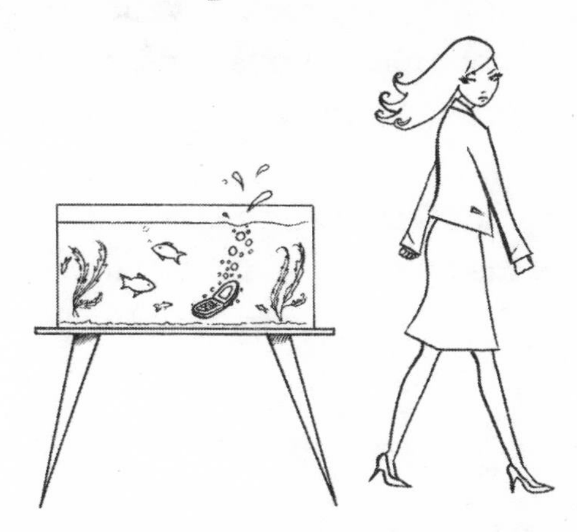

Distraction Management
Part One – Groundwork

We are all animals. We all have needs.

Our friends require entertainment; your dating games will fulfil this obligation. Good sex comes when you are content with the good life you have created for yourself. There is nothing wrong in having a Distraction or Object, as long as they make you smile. There is a danger, of course, that these Objects can make you feel anything but content, and then they need to be ditched.

This chapter will focus on identifying your target and how to lay the groundwork for a romance, your primary tool in this process being telecommunications. These may be the bane of the modern day SG's life; however, mastering them is the name of the game.

The early stages of an involvement can on some levels be compared to the process that the manager of a sports team goes through.

Selection

There is a mathematical formula for the socially acceptable age range for your Distraction. For older, double your age and minus seven. For younger, half your age and add seven. Thus, if you are 28, you are allowed to go up to 49 and down to 21. There are obviously numerous other factors – from bedroom compatibility to breeding agendas – but if you are pushing either side of the formula, you need to dismiss the Distraction directly, since it is distasteful. This will not stop some men getting very strange ideas; a man a year younger than my father, and considerably over my maximum, once lunged at me. I suspect I will remain in shock until my dying day. By the same token, my SG contemporaries have had boys under the age of 18 try it on – when we were at least ten years older than they. Bless the little jailbaits' cotton socks.

It is also advisable to play with someone who is sure enough in himself to measure up to you – and you to him. It is not about social class or job, it is about attitude. A corporate financier girlfriend of mine has had her most successful relationship in recent times with an impoverished waiter/actor who she met at a gig. Despite this, he has the confidence to give as good as he gets, and they work similar hours. She tried to date an accountant with a similar wage packet to her own, but he was a nine to fiver and got needy when she was still in the office at 11 p.m. Be honest with yourself about the type of man who you will play the best possible – and fairest – game with. I once dated an extremely handsome and successful man, a real alpha male, the sort who could have any model of perfection at his beck and call. It was doomed. I felt he was out of my league and simply was too hung up about my cellulite around him to be happy, and he spent too much time and cash grooming himself for my taste. He subsequently went on to have a long-term relationship with a glamorous thespian, whilst I misjudged things and went for his complete opposite – a division three man of dubious attractiveness who was unable to banter back – he was a bit of a slow sentence former. You need to be with someone who you can frolic with on an equal footing.

If you do decide to play with fire and go for a legendary Lothario, it is essential you keep the matter in perspective and not to tie yourself in knots trying to make what can only be a fling last forever. I have a text relationship with a man who makes the previous alpha male look like a Sunday village league footballer – this Distraction actually adorned my wall in smouldering repose on posters I tore from *Just Seventeen* as an overweight teenager with a monobrow. True to cliché, he is shorter in real life than on the screen, but still had an unmistakable magnetism on the night we met in a very dimly lit bar (thank God – he would not have given me a second glance in daylight, I was having a serious skin shocker). However, if you are going to flirt with a Jack Nicholson type, then you need to have a realistic attitude. I have no intention of falling for Mr Alpha ++ – trying to tame him would be a hiding to nothing – but the fun is in the flirtation. His first text will forever remain the most exciting of my life, and I have saved it on three phones.

For karma's sake, only knowingly select unattached males out of principle. Not only will some girl nick your other half at some point if you make a habit of stealing other peoples' boys, but if the Object can deceive a fellow female to give you one, should he ever abandon her (unlikely when he is munching his apple pie and shagging it as well), you will never know for sure that he will not deceive you too. Yes, it can be tempting – my perfect man happens to be very married. I will absolutely never touch him – I am a child of divorce, I am not going to be a cause of it. If a man wants to be with you, he will move mountains to do so.

Emotions are hard to account for; who is to say that the silent, smouldering sort in the corner of the club is not your knight-in-slightly-tarnished-armour? However, in your heart of hearts you will swiftly recognise him for what he is. For a fling, nothing can beat the enthusiasm of the younger man. For something more stable, the slightly older man called Neil will do the trick. I jest not; I have yet to encounter a man called Neil who does not make for anything other than a dull but reliable boyfriend. Remember *Dirty Dancing*? The short man trying to kiss Baby who had three hotels was called Neil – they are a type. Neils also make superb lawyers and accountants for the same reason.

All prospective Distractions should be given facetious nicknames, such as 'Trevor' or 'Wayne' for when you are discussing them with your friends, as this will help you keep your perspective and stop boys from undermining you, which they can have the ability to do all too well. A 'Nigel' was awful to me, but I gained smug satisfaction every time I used his nickname with my girlfriends – giving him a moniker he would have loathed quickened the healing process, reducing his importance to that of a small flea. If the Distractions are actually called such names, seriously reconsider dating them at all. It may not be their fault, but their parents chose these awful appellations and they will have moulded them in some unfortunate way. Alternatively, you can christen them according to strange habits – I had 'Woof Boy', who thought it was endearing to text me the word 'woof' – I am at a loss to explain why, although I am sure some would say I look like a canine from certain angles. He deserved the designation; not only was he patronising in the extreme but he only found women attractive if they weighed in at the size zero zone of under fifty kilos. I did at the time, but I was also seriously ill with a thyroid problem. The added advantage of this type of label is that it aids friends in remembering who you are referring to – one girlfriend has 'Ping Pong Boy', someone who takes part in the sport at organised competitive level and whose conversation is as tedious as his chosen recreational pursuit. If she brings him up by his real name I can never remember which of her suitors she is referring to. When the specimens are really dreadful, we do not even bother thinking up new nicknames, they have to share them – thus there is a 'Woof Boy II' and a 'Woof Boy in Training'.

At the pre-kissing stage, when you are just collecting nominations, it is absolutely acceptable to have more than one interest – the heavyweight challenge, middleweight match and lightweight pushover. If you have more than one prospective Distraction, any rejection on their part becomes amusing, and you play a much better, cooler game with all of them. Because you are juggling so many, you are less likely to stalk. You can almost guarantee that you will not be the only girl on the Distraction's radar – this is men we are talking about here, all you are doing is levelling the playing field.

Game Plan

You are attending events in superior SG style, with CLs, business cards and phone at the ready – and a Wingman in tow who will disappear at a signal's notice. You are thus by default putting yourself in harm's way, with the possibility of meeting a potential Distraction and exchanging details. You are almost there.

It may sound obvious, but it has been known to elude one or two SGs of my acquaintance that if you identify a possible Object at a gathering, make yourself known to them. Men are not mind-readers. One SG friend always bemoans the fact that she is single, but when she finds a man she likes, she will ignore him. There is shy, and there is self-foot-shooting. Locate a mutual friend to make the introduction – you do not have to make your interest that obvious, just say to the introducer, 'I'm sure I've seen that man over there somewhere before at a work thing... what's his name again?', and they will no doubt take you over to this month's potential Distraction. Alternatively, catch his eye for a moment too long, and if he does not come to you, brush past him later whilst talking loudly to your Wingman about an inane subject he can easily interject on, for instance, 'I'm hungry' (good double entendre potential), 'Crowded in here tonight', 'No, you cannot possibly equate Daniel Craig's performance as Bond to

George Lazenby's'. Once initial contact is made, your conversation is not rocket science – ask him why he is there, what he does, look at his wedding ring finger. If all is flowing nicely perhaps mention a film you wish to view or new bar you would like to sample. Allow him a way in.

If digits are still not looking close to being exchanged, steer the talk round to MySpace to see if he has a page and say you should both connect as friends, or mention an amusing e-mail forward he just has to see, and then give him your card. A man needs some encouragement, but if there is a smidgen of interest on his part, he will take the bait, and your number. If he is proving hard to hook, move on – you spend a lot of time in the sea and know there are a lot of fish in it.

Some sort of contact mechanism exchanged, we move onto the trickiest part of groundwork. We now need to get the targeted Distraction to agree to play where we want them, and in the style that will suit our game. In today's world, there is only one way to do this – by e-mail and phone.

The Bennet sisters of yesteryear had it easy. Courtship etiquette in the nineteenth century had nothing on the perils of trying to pull using modern day communication. In centuries gone by, the scenarios the protagonists faced were so much less challenging. There were plain, established rules, and by and large they were stuck to.

From the female perspective, perhaps you had a little too much wine with your six course feast and when the men retired you confided to your fellow lady guests – including a wise old aunt who you knew would manipulate the situation into marriage – about your feelings for your chosen one. You then floated up to bed. The worst case scenario was that on decorseting yourself you felt sufficiently released from etiquette's constricted bounds to write a late night love letter. However, on awaking the following morning you realised how foolish revealing your hand in such an undignified manner would have been – and you burnt it.

There were natural safety mechanisms in place in previous millennia. If the man in question had penned a rather too honest missive after a slight overindulgence with the port, he too would have had the chance to censor himself the next day. As a result, the apple of his eye would never have awoken next to him the following morning having done something she should not, and he would not have run a mile in the opposite direction as his thirst for that wench had been quenched. Alternatively, the scenario would not have arisen whereby she had made the mistake of fornicating with a man whose looks in daylight were not so much brooding as bad-tempered. In times gone by there was an intrinsic slower rhythm to courting that just meant the whole business was less reckless.

Even twenty years ago, it was easier. E-mail and mobiles were primitive, obscure things that few people used, let alone abused. Not so now. The progress in modern technology has had the unfortunate side effect of our courting world becoming one never-ending fast-paced battle, rejection and romancing done at a speed that our ancestors never had to cope with. It has been the final nail in the coffin of innocence.

For in today's society, you go out, you imbibe far too much alcohol, invariably on an empty stomach because you worked late, and decide it is a wise move to get candid. With the clarity that only cocktails can bring, you make a booty text or call. Perhaps, because you have online access at home when you totter back from an evening out, or indeed possess a Blackberry, you write a badly spelt and grammatically incorrect epic e-mail to the Object of your affection.

Rarely is the result of such communications a fortuitous conclusion. The nightmare, and often predictable, plot is that the Object does not respond to your proposal. Even worse, is that he subsequently tells, indeed forwards, the epistle to all his friends. If the boot were on the other foot, you would not hesitate to reveal the contents of the booty communication, would you?

Alternatively, he immediately answers your entreaty or indeed makes the text or calls himself, and you invite him round. You without fail stir the next morning with a sore head and un-boy-proofed skin and flat, wondering whether you were the first person on his list. One impish Italian man of my acquaintance regularly texts me 'Ciao Bella' at 3 a.m. Fortunately I have never taken him up on his approaches – invariably when I compare notes with mutual female friends the next day it becomes apparent that they were contacted too. We SGs have actually deduced there are distinct patterns to his overtures, and believe he must have set up group distribution lists, which he contacts depending on his mood – 'Blonde', 'Brunette' and 'European'.

It is not that the present day situation is entirely bleak; used correctly, mobiles and computers can reel in the prey in a marvellous manner. However, it is far too easy to screw up texts and e-mails and to sabotage even the most promising fledgling relationship. Computers and mobiles should come with warning labels attached: 'this equipment could ruin your life'. Otherwise they should have built-in safeguards – e-mails to certain people are unable to go out without twenty-four hours in a 'pending' box, and are then sent round to a number of friends to veto before finally being sent. Texts and calls should operate on the same basis.

But they do not. And until they do, we have to deal with the all out warfare that is courting in the twenty-first century. I write these words of wisdom and warning with the bitter experience of someone who has seriously mismanaged all these tools in the past.

The Computer

From a personal perspective, the rot set in – in more ways than one – at university. I got into the habit of checking my e-mail on my way to/from the College bar, even being known to interrupt my alcopops for a swift login during the evening. Consequently, whilst a sprite and supple student, there began the era of the heart stopping, hung-over checking of my 'sent mail' folder the following day. However, e-mail does have its uses. It was during this unfortunate university period that I discovered a despicable, but essential, tool to the modern courter's repertoire. The funny or useful forward e-mail, also known as 'the BCC'.

The BCC

The Blind Carbon Copy (BCC), where those who receive an e-mail do not know who else the sender has dispatched it to, is an essential tool that almost every single person with access to a computer knows about, and if they do not, they should – they are liable to have been subjected to manipulation by someone and been ignorant of it. I do not have a single friend who has not been guilty of using the BCC at some point in their existence. Indeed, the BCC is no longer just a way of copying undisclosed recipients in on an e-mail, and instead has come to be a reason for sending an e-mail in itself.

The BCC normally takes the form of a 'funny forward' or some essential information such as a change of e-mail address – indeed my GBF has on occasion got a new e-mail address just so as to be able to BCC a special someone. Ostensibly it prevents some joker from 'replying all' and cluttering up everyone's e-mails with boring banter. However, it also provides an excuse to get in touch with someone indirectly, and hence saves embarrassment if they do not respond. Unlike with a direct e-mail or a text or call, there is less loss of face as it is socially acceptable not to reply to a BCC.

By sending a BCC, you are reminding the other party of your existence and:

a) you want to let them know it is OK they did not text you back (or heaven forbid call)
b) you want them to text/call
c) you are saying 'let bygones be bygones'
d) all of the above.

Confused? So you should be. The BCC is all about mixed messages, indeed it could be about sending no subliminal message at all, which is why it is so useful. The BCC has become a widespread phenomenon and for a girl trying to subtly encourage a boy to ask her out without being too obvious, and therefore off-putting in overture, it is a far more useful device than a mobile, a modern day cupid's arrow if you will. Men like to chase, to feel in control, and they still can if you have sent them a BCC, you have just let them know that you are amenable to approach. On several occasions, including with Mr Alpha ++, I have actually gone to the trouble of getting Objects to text me their e-mail address, when I only have their mobile number, making up an excuse about an e-mail I need to send them, just so I have this extra weapon at my disposal.

At which point, it is important to note a number of caveats about the tactic. The first thing is, quadruple check that you have put the Object (or Objects – it can be fun to send the e-mail to all men you have crushes on and see who responds) on the BCC line. My GBF once managed to send a BCC round to all the boys he liked and loathed, but put them on the CC line by mistake. No girls, no friends, just boys that everyone knew he had slept with or wanted to. It was an utter disaster. The GBF never kissed any of them again and could not prance down Old 'Condom' Compton Street in Soho for at least a week for the humiliation.

If you know your Object's friends, include them on the BCC – you then ensure the e-mail will not be identified as too contrived if your Object brings up the fact you have e-mailed him alone about something ostensibly general, such as a 'save-the-date' for your forthcoming S&M party. You may want to whip him into shape on your own, but it will be a little subtler if others are invited too. Remember, the BCC is about sparing your blushes – you are merely sending out an e-mail to many friends, and on no account is it a mantrap, oh no.

Your selection of the actual content of the forward is crucial. Do try to send something that is funny or useful or makes you look busy/popular/important. If it is from a stockpile (the prepared modern girl has a 'funny' e-mail folder for moments such as this), remember to double check you have not sent it out to them before and remove the header from the previous sender. The BCC is all about illusion, and it does not look great if you are forwarding an e-mail dredged up from March and it is now June the following year.

You could also always put a standard 'signature' on your forward as well, so they have all your details. I have gone on a number of dates after men have put to good use the numbers I list accidentally-on-purpose at the end of my e-mails.

The time of day you send the missive is key. Lunchtime is a good time for a BCC, since it is a perfectly natural time to remember your friends. Before 10 a.m. is too premeditated, and is liable to be ignored by the contact as he will not have yet had enough coffee to apply himself to anything other than work. Never send a BCC after 7 p.m.; you should be out playing, doing something or someone better then sending ridiculous e-mails to males. Remember – the BCC is the bait, and you need to keep up appearances.

Of course the risk is that he does not reply. However, if you have taken the steps above, you should have minimised your humiliation. If he fails to respond, do not slit your wrists – he was obviously busy. If he really is enamoured, he will always reply, and several increasingly flirty e-mails later you will have hooked him.

The Direct E-mail

If you must directly e-mail, and when chasing a man who really has not wanted me I have resorted to this tactic, try to make it short and to contain a pertinent question that only he can give you a suitable reply to. For example, something in his area of work expertise or what to buy a very good mutual friend for their birthday. One particular girlfriend of mine actually drafts e-mails to her Objects, then sends them on to me to edit. We had to introduce this rule after she e-mailed an amour before their second date asking whether it was time their parents met – her stalker status was not only assured, but one step away from a restraining order. Now, when she finally e-mails them out, she BCC's me so that I am kept abreast of the situation.

The question mark is a key indicator of where the parties stand when directly e-mailing. It is rude not to reply to an e-mail with a question mark in it. The keener party, the sender, knows this, and will therefore utilise one. The respondent is interested if they in turn insert a question mark into their reply. If they do not reply, give up. Either they are useless at e-mailing and will do something constructive like call you later, or they just do not want to kiss you.

A word of warning on direct e-mailing. One notorious playboy cautions to never send an e-mail with the subject heading 'Hey'. He literally shivered as he said it whilst his fingers motioned hitting a keyboard's delete button. Such a title immediately puts him on the back foot, as it indicates that the contents of the e-mail will be needling, invariably trying to elicit a date or girlfriend status from him.

As with the BCC, pick your moment for the direct e-mail. If you know he is going to be hung-over, try for 11.30 a.m. – he will be counting down the minutes to sandwich buying time and craving sympathy for his crashing headache.

He-mail Banter

So, you have BCC'd or directly e-mailed him, and he has got back to you (even better/easier if he has BCC'd or directly e-mailed first, but modern boys are lazy and often need a smidgen of encouragement). A reply within minutes is a very good sign, as this is an invitation to indulge in He-mail banter. There is no substitute for experience here and it is a tough call to make. Some advocate playing hard to get and waiting for a few hours before replying. However, a rapid succession of funny, flirty e-mails may just obtain you the date you are trying to engineer.

It is important to develop a regular sign-off in e-mails. Mine used to be 'Lots of love' followed by three kisses. This scared off one suitor who did not realise it was standard. I have now gone for my initial, 'I', followed by one little kiss. If I put just kisses, and lots of them, this is someone I like. If I am worried about encouraging someone I am not into, I lose the kisses completely.

Take the tone of your sign-off from him. If he is leaning on the 'x' button and you really like him, you can too, but always make sure you send slightly fewer kisses, and never more. If you want to keep caveman interested, he has to labour under the impression he is chasing you.

Remember e-mails can be forwarded and recorded. Just ask Claire Swire, the poor girl who e-mailed her Object a graphic description of how much she had enjoyed an intimate interlude with him, and it went worldwide like wildfire. E-mail sex can be unbelievably hot, but you are then living in fear. Forever.

Some computer systems and websites have Instant Messenger (IM), where you can see targets online and instantly connect with them so a message pops up on their screen. IM is a dreadful invention unless you are in a relationship and having IM sex. Otherwise, it has nothing to commend it whatsoever – you are inevitably got when you are actually busy at work. Never, ever, ever, IM a boy first. Boys really do have one-track minds and can only do one thing at a time, so imagine how he will feel if he is actually in the middle of something vital. I can multitask, and it even drives me to distraction. IM is simply inappropriate. One lovely boy who I would have been completely wrong for (he refused to believe that I did not share his ambition to move from London to a place where you cultivate cabbages instead of hailing them) declared undying love on IM. It was in the middle of an IM conversation that he had started and I did not want to be involved with anyway, as I was getting all taxed by my tax return. Talk about putting me on the spot – he can see I am online, I cannot go anywhere. After a panic-stricken online silence, I opted for the laughing it off option and treated the declaration as a joke, almost saving the faces of everyone involved, until a member of his IT department, who had been monitoring the exchange, decided to forward the transcript around his company. Such 'big brotherly' love.

Bouncing Unwanted Males

Some males need to get the message that you are simply not interested. Attempt not to resort to rudeness unless you really have to – remember how you would feel if you were in their position and treat them as you would be treated. Also recall that these chasers have a purpose: we all need the ego-boost boys – they help negate the ego-battering variety.

The rules to get rid of such a boy are simple – flip the tips above. Never send him a BCC; never respond if he e-mails you one. And if he sends you an e-mail with a question, although it is only polite to get back to him, leave your response for a few days and do not include a question of your own. If he instant messages you, say that you are sorry but you are manic and need to go, then shut the IM window.

Eventually he will get the message. Otherwise, call the courts.

The Internet

Forget being a research tool for scientists, the Internet was clearly invented to investigate potential conquests, and if you are lucky, yours will have some cyberspace listings. The crafty courter will use tools such as Google, MySpace, Facebook and aSmallWorld. These devices can be exceptionally helpful, not only when working out the right questions to ask, but also when gauging at what level you should pitch your interest in, for instance, the rise of eco-friendly big business. They can also aid establishing whether or not it is worth spending any time with prospective Distractions, since they can reveal skeletons in the closet or current attachments.

Once, out on the prowl with my GBF, we met a beautiful boy, the only one we have ever competed for. We both thrust out our chests, pushed our shoulders back, and launched ourselves on him, dribbling so much that pools of saliva formed at our feet. I won the battle, and the man in question spent four weeks trying to track down my phone number – I had had to let him leave without giving it to him as his parents had suddenly materialised by his side. In a fit of jealousy, the GBF decided to tease me that the gorgeous boy was years younger than me – that I was venturing into cradle-snatching, rather than boy toy, territory – after all, he was out with his mother. One Google search and some laboured mental arithmetic later, I realised that my new Object was, in fact, thirteen months older, and I was absolutely allowed to date him.

The Google image search can also be invaluable if you met them whilst marginally merry in a darkened room. Thanks to the explosion of MySpace and the like, many a male has pictures, if not a blog, online. It is important to remember, however, that information gleaned from a web search may be incorrect. One of my male confidants shares a name with a porn star. Although my friend has been notorious for his promiscuity in the past, and videoing his nocturnal activities is not something his friends would put past him, it is not he. If I Google myself, a pile of incorrect information (my publisher got worried when I was listed somewhere as seven years old – were they doing a deal with a child?), not to mention some very dubious photos, appears.

It is not a good look to reveal that you have Googled. Ever. Doing an Internet search on a prospect is a bit like the BCC – everyone knows it is there, everybody does it, but nobody admits to it. My GBF once had a shocker when he was so well-informed about his date that the Object realised he had been Googled, suspected he was out with a stalker, and swiftly swept out of the cocktail lounge. Remember you are not supposed to know this information – let them tell you. Internet research can just allow you to have a very good CL, which with luck will not be required anyway, as the pair of you will be getting on like Johnny and Baby after he fished her out of the corner.

The Internet has, of course, other more transparent options – the online love affair with someone you meet on a blog/dating etc. site. I hold a deep suspicion of starting a relationship with someone I have not actually met. Yes, computers can be used to elicit dates, but from my experiences, described in Chapter Five, it does truly help if you have some real-life knowledge of what the other party involved looks like first. No one is going to be honest if they write a description of themselves – they will suddenly come over all accomplished, and any photo they select is going to be dimly lit and photoshopped enough to imply that they are more Leonardo DiCaprio than Laurence Llewellyn-Bowen.

Dating a keyboard is dubious. And if you go to meet your online love, take backup, and keep your phone handy.

The Mobile Phone

Freud would have needed decades to analyse the havoc this small device has caused to our society. My mobile is my contact with everyone; it is my business, family, friend, lover and, when the Object's not getting in touch, my enemy. There is no denying it – I absolutely have a relationship with my phone; without it I feel naked, exposed, incomplete. The trauma that losing a phone incurs – the missing numbers, texts and photos – is a nightmare not to bear thinking about.

When I get my annual upgrade it is a massive decision over which new model will be mine. Then there is the cleansing process – only a certain number of names and texts can transfer on my SIM card to the new phone. From business contacts to boyfriends – who's in, who's out? Which texts do I leave behind? Which lovers do I finally close the book on? Changing phones causes me to reflect on my life more than any birthday does. The mobile has become the modern day person's version of a journal, where sinful secrets and mundane matters are stored. (Suspicious other halves no longer need sneak a peek at the diary, just the phone.) For all SGs the phone is the most intimate point of contact with the Object besides being in his presence. It is where his tender texts are saved, where his calls at 3 a.m. appear in 'call records'.

The mobile phone game is high roller territory and as such the stakes are highly speculative and there is the ever-present risk that you can lose everything. However, there are some steps you can take to minimise the threat of having to declare yourself a love bankrupt.

An early procedure to implement with your mobile is to organise your address book. Make sure the telephone numbers of exes or current interests are not the first number in your Contacts section or stored near taxi numbers/BFs. As one male Lothario of my acquaintance says, 'Everyone needs an Aardvark.' An accident will happen – almost everyone has a sob story that is the result of an inept listing. A girlfriend was doing very well in ignoring a man who was bad for her. She had managed not to contact him for weeks and disregarded all his attempts at communication, until one day she accidentally dropped her phone and it rang the first name in her contact book – his. It was a catastrophe. She ended up getting back with him, then having an even more traumatic break-up several months later.

When you have an Object's number safely stored, you should then allocate him his own ring and message tones (although remember to switch them onto vibrate when you are with people who might tell him or, quite rightly, laugh). I have returned new phones before on discovering that they do not have these functions. It saves endless agony of hoping it is him when your phone makes a noise, then finding that it is just something unimportant, like your bank manager querying a large purchase from a shoe shop.

These are all ways to make this compulsory courting tool more bearable, yet, like the computer, the mobile can be manipulated to help the predator trap his prey. However, it is a difficult weapon to command, and not even the masters or mistresses of the mobile will get it right all the time – even though we know we should not drink and dial, accidents can, and do, happen.

The Text Message

There are two types of people in the world. Those who almost always respond immediately to all texts (me) and those who do not (the majority of the population, apparently). You will very quickly ascertain which one your Object is, and you must adjust your behaviour accordingly. There are some golden rules, however, in the text game.

- Try never to be last to text. This really is not a good look.The old saying, 'leave them wanting more' is definitely true. If it is unavoidable, so be it, but remember it looks especially bad if you are the one who instigated the exchange.

- Do not double text – so do not be last and then first to text again with a new subject unless there is a very good reason. Wanting to know how they are doing, or to tell them that you miss them is not a good enough reason. If you are ever tempted to double text, please call your friends first and consult. Then refrain.

- Kisses in texts, as in e-mails, are a minefield. If in doubt, put a smiley face instead of a kiss. Or just leave it. If he puts two kisses it means you are in business.

- Big letters mean shouting. Make them little unless you are joking or very cross indeed.

- Like e-mail, if you want a reply to a text, put a question mark, otherwise recipients can ignore them. If they neglect to reply at this point, it is not disastrous if they are the sort who never text back. But it is not looking good if they are normally of nimble thumb.

- If you know you are liable to text the Object, but that it is crucial that you do not, brief some friends and then text them instead when you are struck by an overwhelming need to contact him. Sometimes it is just a case of keeping your fingers and phone busy to prevent a communications error. If needs be, give your mobile to someone else to look after until the moment has passed, or write the Object's number down and delete it off your phone – it will make you think twice about texting if you have to locate it and type it in.

On the whole, I try not to day text Monday to Friday. There is always e-mail, which is less invasive and permissible (at certain times, see above) during working hours and if a boy is in full professional flow he will not take too kindly to being interrupted. If you must day text, do not expect an immediate response and try to leave at least ten minutes before replying if he texts you – you have far more weighty things to attend to.

After 6 p.m., however, it is a whole different ball game. Answers can be immediate – it is about flirtatious repartee. There are some tactics for evening hours, but we are in a risky, winner-takes-all contest, with possible humiliation lurking around the corner with every move.

There does exist the mobile phone equivalent of the BCC – the 'group' text, where you send out the same text to a number of contacts. This is a device to be used only sparingly and if you do not have his e-mail address, or if it is over New Year when nobody attractive should have e-mail access. Unlike the BCC, your options are very limited for the group text. 'Happy New Year' is fine; texting your birthday arrangements, again OK. I have delved as low as a 'who's playing tonight?' but that was quite frankly embarrassing. It worked, but the abashment lasted longer than the liaison.

I am a fan of textual healing – a quick note to get a relationship back on track, whether it be a friendship endangered by an accidental kiss or an argument you need to apologise for. I always send these communications early evening or at weekends, at a time the recipient knows I must be sober, and that they are not in fact some sort of veiled bed-beckoning transmission.

In helping develop a situation with an Object, an empathetic text about their hangover the day after you have seen them out on the town and know that they are going to be feeling rough can work wonders. Men like sympathy, so if they are suffering 'man flu' aka a runny nose, a 'get well soon' text will also no doubt reach appreciative thumbs.

There is also the strategy of mistakenly sending a text to someone on purpose. You and your friends know that you would never send a text in error as you have arranged your phone book listings accordingly; however, your latest Object will not. You could therefore send a text making yourself look busy and in demand – for example, 'So sorry, am running late, but will be there soon... x' and send it to him. If he gets back to you, apologise – in your haste you mistakenly texted the Object rather than your friend above him in your listings. This is a regular ploy for a gay friend of mine, with stellar results, although use it sparingly, as it is a bit obvious.

We now enter the high-risk zone – the booty text, the late night emergence of a message in your Object's trousers. If you are going to perform a late night booty text, try and make it relatively subtle (as subtle as a text sent after midnight can be) so as to avoid next day/week/year/lifelong humiliation. Perhaps you have seen him out or know he is going out, in which case – as long as he knows that you have not set your alarm at midnight so you wake up to send the text especially, and you are actually out yourself – 'Hope your head doesn't hurt tomorrow x' is a relatively safe one. This gives them a window of opportunity to get in touch at 3 a.m. saying they want to come round for some nocturnal activity. If they do not, they are just left with an aching head the following day and a sympathetic message. 'I want you now big boy' does not work as well when they have woken up next to another girl feeling like death, but very pleased with themselves all the same – it will merely serve to inflate their ego all the more, even if a certain part of their anatomy is a temporarily deflated force.

3G phones are hideous inventions, their downside far outweighing their upside. Please try not to send pictures or videos of yourself naked. He will either lose the phone, his friends will steal it, or he will show pictures of you naked to them anyway. Just ask Charlotte Church about Gavin Henson's stolen mobile.

Hopefully you will soon get past the text message obstacle course of a stage – if a man wants to conduct a relationship almost always by virtual means of communication and rarely sees you, then he is **all text no trousers** and the little **Clit Teaser** needs to be sent on his way. Real romances require the exchange of bodily fluids.

Calling

Unless you are in a relationship, do not call. Like barbecuing, it is one of the few jobs that remain for the male species, and it is wrong to deprive them of it. Text is sufficient for the female – girls have a tendency to be useless on the phone to boys anyway. According to one predatory male, girls should never leave voicemails – they get flustered and humiliate themselves. It is not as if there is a need to leave one anyway – if you do call, he can see 'missed calls', the modern equivalent of calling cards. If he never calls back, he is call screening; take the hint.

Keep in mind that if a man wants you, he will find his way to you. If he fails to e-mail, text or call, his computer and phone may be broken or stolen. He could also be in Switzerland, whereby because of their '079' phone-codes, amorous texts and calls can end up in the wrong place if you are there and using a UK mobile. One man I know almost ditched his girl because he called her from the slopes and another man answered – turns out he had forgotten to add '+44' and had got a random Swiss. However, if a man wants you and one type of communication fails, at some point in the near future he will try another. If it has proper potential, meeting should really not be that hard. Thus we turn to the next step.

The date.

Chapter Eight

Distraction Management Part Two – Kissing etc.

The pre-match deliberations are over, you have made your selection; it is now time to play the game itself.

At all stages keep in mind why you are putting yourself through these sometimes exhausting encounters: entertainment. However tough it may be out there on the field, you are there because of the enjoyment your friends will obtain from the debrief the following day, and the anecdotes that you can subsequently regale people with forevermore because of the rendezvous. And you may also get some kissing out of it.

This chapter is about the physical interaction you have with your Distractions, from dates to the exchange of bodily fluids. At all times you need to keep in mind one word: fun. For if the exchanges you are having with your Object do not have a frisson of fun about them, then what is the point? These initial moments with him (or her, we touch on bisexuality too) are supposed to be the delicious stage – and if they are not you need to get out of the entanglement and start the selection process again as soon as possible.

The Date

The Proposition

A proper Distraction is one that you see in person, that you go on a date with. Now 'date' is a loose, informal, unofficial, term; you could just be hanging out at each other's places – or you could be being swept off your Choo clad feet (a pre-rendezvous present, naturally) and into a Venetian gondola. However, if any or all of the following instances occur – you are alone with a boy you like, you shave your legs, you wear matching underwear, you boy-proof your flat, you alert friends to the meeting's occurrence – we are calling it a date.

The definition of date may encompass a lot, but not everything. If your Distraction has brought friends to talk to and ignores you, he is not interested. I once turned up to what I thought would be a romantic dinner, and instead we 'accidentally bumped into' two of my Object's male friends, who he then insisted join us. This heavy-handed and unsubtle method of protection lacked finesse, but then we were barely out of our teens at the time, and I have subsequently come across men who execute this manoeuvre with admittedly slightly more style, but who carry it out nevertheless. The other scenario to be wary of is any meet-up with your Object that occurs between the hours of 10 p.m.–3 a.m. More than one supremely desirable rake I know adheres to the belief that any dalliance that transpires with any girls during these hours does not count. You do not want to be one of them – you absolutely count.

There may be certain proclivities that are no-go's for you, in which case make your position known early on. Men who do coke are a big turn off for me (apart from anything else, males who hoover can never get it up when you require them to). Within minutes of meeting a potential someone I will therefore have relayed an amusing anecdote that states my position in no uncertain terms. It is sad but true that for most SG friends of mine, more than one relationship has stalled because the man is already in one with one too many substances.

On the flip side, there seem to be a growing number of men who are completely clean. I recently went to a singles dinner party where none of the men were drinking and all the girls were (in moderation, but we suddenly felt like the hardest partyers on the planet – or that we were in LA). Be wary of extremes. The abstinence may simply indicate that your Distraction is driving, which of course means they must refrain; it could be that they are health freaks, in which case it would help if you are too; or it might be that they are in recovery for addiction to something slightly more potent than a skinny moccachino. Of the four men at this particular dinner only one was driving; the rest had issues. Such addictions should be flagged up and considered carefully early on, so you do not even dip your toe in the water if you feel the current will be too strong for you to cope with.

Once you have settled on your target, in a casual (but let's face it, probably contrived) manner, over text, e-mail or even conversation banter, there is the suggestion you meet with the Object and actually do something together. Occasionally, you may find yourself agreeing to a date with someone who is not necessarily your idea of an ideal male. It could be that you end up accepting a mercy date – a man has pursued you so much and got mutual friends to beg on his behalf to such an extent that it becomes rude not to give him his chance. Or it could be accidental – I have agreed before to a date on Instant Messenger because I was concentrating on work, rather than the cyber conversation. Whatever the case, suggestions on how to cope with these scenarios follow.

A word of warning for those who are prone to not leaving their house if the daily Horrorscope texted to their phone says they are in for an inauspicious day. In the run up to the date, I know it is tempting whilst in the supermarket checkout queue to sneak a little look at your and his star signs in each magazine you pass. However, they are not useful for anything other than wrist slitting. One SG I know actually went against her better judgement and followed a Horrorscope that said she was destined to fall in love with someone she met near a red door. Whilst at a house party – the front door was red – a man asked her out and she agreed. Mutual acquaintances were agog; he was known as duller than dishwater whilst she is as sparky as a sparkler. On their first date, Dishwater Man lived up to his reputation and proceeded to take Miss Sparkle though about two hundred of his holiday snaps, before asking her to choose her three favourites. There was no second date, but he took months to get the message, sending a succession of e-mails with the subject heading 'Hey'. I sense collective SG shuddering after the lessons learned of Chapter Seven.

The Setting

The male species still like to labour under the misapprehension that they are in the driver's seat over the arrangements of a date even when they are not – so let them. In selecting the venue, allow him to suggest, but if necessary steer him towards what you find acceptable.

If the date was arranged under duress or accidentally, then opt to meet them in daylight and have lunch or coffee – dinner *à deux* in a notoriously romantic restaurant is not yet what the doctor ordered, if ever. If by some miracle you and your companion do get on, you can then up the location ante on subsequent meetings, but for now, if you suspect that the man is the type where you have lots to say *for a lunch*, keep it to that. If a waiter sees a couple for dinner, they may assume you want to linger, and slow the service accordingly – this is not ideal. There will be no such error pre-6 p.m., when you will be in and out within an hour.

For the slightly better prospect, someone perhaps you are in two minds about, meet for drinks; if you are getting on famously you can then go on to dinner, and if not, you can go and join Bunbury. For all early dating scenarios, until you know what kind of Distraction you are dealing with, ensure the Distraction knows all about the unfortunate Bunbury and their unpredictable demands on your time. Bunbury can always cancel on you halfway through the evening (you will have primed friends to text you at appropriate points) so you are suddenly at a loose end and your Distraction can rescue you from the predicament of a gap in your social schedule in knight-in-dining-armour fashion.

Your Distraction's behaviour during the planning stage of the date will indicate a good deal about him. If he takes control, listens to your preferences, and then arranges something wonderful having thought everything through, then this is probably someone you want to spend time with. If he is indecisive and picks a venue which serves food that would not be out of place in a 'bushtucker trial', the early indicators are not great. However, although your initial instinct may be to cancel the encounter altogether, do remember that until you have actually spent time with him you cannot be sure how things will pan out – a fair player should give an Object a sporting chance. My BF had a boyfriend who suggested a first date location of bowling. Not only is this the type of activity that she loathes – audience participation is not her thing; she likes to be entertained, not be the entertainment – she also disliked the tactic whereby your shoes are taken from you so you cannot run away. Before she fled from meeting with him at all, a Platonic Boyfriend pointed out that at least he was showing initiative and neither suggesting a paltry pint and packet of crisps at the local nor delegating the arrangements to her. The BF tactfully suggested an activity more to her liking – a picnic – and love almost blossomed with the birds and the bees, until both types of wildlife got over-amorous with their food and caused this bird and bee to find refuge… in the nearest pub.

If the choice of venue is left in your hands, it is unwise in the early dating stages to rendezvous with your Object at a meeting place that you regularly frequent with friends. If it all goes pear-shaped, you will never be able to return to your favourite pub/bar/restaurant without fear of bumping into him; naturally your taste is so good he will attempt to steal your stomping grounds. Early on in my dating career I was careless enough to do this, and after running into the man more times than I cared to, I was forced to change my playgrounds.

The Costume

Once the venue is selected, make sure your outfit matches accordingly – football matches do not require Fendi, unless your date is Roman Abramovich, or works in the football 'industry'. I was once fortunate enough to be taken to a match by an insider, who kindly informed me that we would be sitting in the director's box and that 'we dress a little differently there'. Unfortunately for him I used an episode of *Footballers' Wives* as a reference point – I am not sure he has ever got over the embarrassment of arriving at the stadium with a girl whose skin was a distinctly Sleazy-Jet shade of orange on his arm.

The Object's attire is equally significant. A man can be too **Metrosexual** – having a Distraction who spends more time and disposable income on shoe shopping than you is just distressing. By the same token, a **Retrosexual** – a male who comes over all caveman and is inordinately proud of his scruffiness and lack of grooming habits – can be just as disagreeable. One lawyer SG friend invited an Object to a Christmas party of one of her clients, an oil firm. To make a stand for the environment, the strict veggie (unless he was hung-over and smelt sizzling bacon) PC type decided to turn up unshaven, in plastic shoes and a pungent fleecy jacket that she suspected had once been mustard in colour, but was now a turd-like shade of brown. My friend had to ditch him on her doorstep and call up her GBF for emergency suited-and-booted Wingman support.

The Banter

Your CL will certainly contain questions pertinent to your Object, as it is useful to find out his views to ascertain whether he is worth spending any more of your time with or not. Since men like talking about themselves, this should be no hardship for them, although it may be for you. One SG had to endure a three-hour dinner date during which the Distraction spent the whole time talking about himself. By the end of the evening, he still did not know what my friend did for a living. To cap it all off, he picked a dome-lifting-tastic pricey restaurant, and after ordering the most expensive champagne and wine on the menu, made her pay half, when aged 22 she did not have the cash. Hell hath no fury – later, at a law firm's dull drinks party, she came across his boss, who asked her opinion of the man.

She let rip about his Scrooge-like people skills; it was the catalyst for him being fired.

Do ascertain your Object's activity levels and interests early; one SG friend is having a lot of fun with a rock climber, as she too possesses a fetish for climbing Snowdon on weekends. Of course it is not compulsory for you to share every pastime – it is healthy to have separate ones – but some will help. I am quite happy for a man to be passionate about footie, as long as he is fine with the arrangement that whilst he is watching men hug each other on a Saturday I am grooming myself with my girlfriends. However, similar mindsets on some matters are useful; if his idea of spending a Sunday is running a marathon whilst your preferred pastime is sex, your differing outlooks may be insurmountable.

Your CL should also be in keeping with the date's venue. Call up a knowledgeable friend if the Object is taking you somewhere that involves an activity he knows a lot about. Never pretend to the target you are an expert – they like to take on that role – but your friend can instruct you on good questions to ask. Research can help, but be wary of anything that you are not directly told. A lovely man once suggested a date to the cinema, which I swiftly accepted, and he left the film selection up to me. I had gleaned from Google that he was into foreign art house films, so picked one of them – and got it so wrong. My source was incorrect, and I had to wake the Distraction up halfway through as he was snoring so loudly. We did a runner, and

I admitted I was just trying to impress him with my cultural leanings (I obviously could not reveal the real, cyber-stalking, reason), and over a bottle of wine we discovered we were both lowbrow movie buffs who prefer their flicks of the blockbuster, Bond variety.

There are some safe, general topics to oil the conversation's wheels if your research exhausts itself or proves inaccurate. Holidays are always a reliable conversation vein – usually people need, have just come back from or are deciding on one. This will aid you in establishing whether you are remotely compatible as well; one potential lover did not even bother to lunge on goodbye once he realised that a mini-break involving me sleeping in a tent on a glacier really was not an option.

The **iPod Icebreaker** is another dependable ploy to employ – ask your date what the most embarrassing song on his iPod is. If they have a sense of humour about it, it is always a good sign, and also the song he chooses will say an awful lot about him. Mine is Boyzone's version of my dad's 'No Matter What'; secret boy band fetish and dad idolisation in one go – no wonder I am single! If you want a snapshot of his deepest, darkest secrets, all you need to do his look at his 'Most Played' playlist – too many show tunes and pass him on to your GBF immediately.

If the date goes spectacularly then you may not have to resort to your CL; however, it is helpful to be prepared and to have one in reserve, as the fear factor can hit any SG's chatter if there is a pair of puppy-dog brown eyes transfixed on her. Conversely you may find yourself in the company of someone exceptionally dull, at which point the CL will make the time flow so much more quickly. If you are controlling the conversation then at least there are no excruciating silences – you will be feeding him the right questions so he will be procrastinating on various topics. Just try to stifle your yawns – though perhaps do not do this too well. One SG girlfriend went on a date with a man who was so dull she used every iota of preparation she had made; he took the pauseless discussion as a sign of their compatibility and spent the next year using his online blog to dedicate soppy, badly spelt poetry to her. She still lives in fear of any Object she actually wants Googling her and finding the lamentable verse.

Demeanour

Clearly your behaviour will alter according to location – life and soul at a bar (although still letting him get his word in edgeways), to quietly contemplative at an art gallery. However, there are some obvious guidelines to adhere to at all times.

Try not to get blindingly drunk. Not only do men find it unattractive, you may also do something you regret. I obviously do not speak from personal experience here, oh no. If you are having drinks, alternate them with water, especially if you will be moving on to wine with dinner later. That's a tip from the top, trust me.

Men like to feel like men, so if at the cinema let them hold the tickets and the popcorn. During the film you can therefore choose whether or not you put your hand in the direction of his crotch area, and with what regularity, as well as ensuring that he is the one more likely to have popcorn stuck all over him when the credits roll.

When it comes to a dinner, do not be put off if he refuses to talk until he has ordered; remember men have one-track minds and they might only be capable of making one decision at a time. Avoid tricky food – if you are eating pasta opt for penne rather than spaghetti, and if you think you may want to kiss him avoid garlic and spring onions, unless he does not. Of course, if you decide you want him nowhere near your personal space, eat as much odoriferous food as you like.

Please eat. SGs who turn up only to traumatise over how they are sacrificing their diet even by ordering just a salad will doubtless have the boy bored into dismissing any off-menu capering with you later quicker than they can say 'I must go find Bunbury'. In general, do try not to get hysterical about food in his presence (one Platonic Boyfriend stopped dating an SG because she was scared of peas and sweetcorn). If some sort of outburst is inevitable, then try to make it endearing. I suffer from 'food rage', intense jealousy of what anyone with me has ordered, so often I will have what he is having, or state early on that I may want a taste of his dish (obviously, exercise caution with that phrase). Sharing can be very sexy;

indeed someone's approach to food is normally a good indicator for something else entirely, and now is the perfect time to assess the potential of those skills.

Gourmands tend to appreciate and know what they are doing in the bedroom, whilst fast eaters are a little too swift in that department and fussy eaters somewhat straight-laced. I am always suspicious if a date eats less than me and refuses to order pudding. How can he be a real man? He must either be doing dinner off the mirror, be bad in bed, or both. An agent I met on a business trip to LA sent me on a blind lunch date. The man in question was a producer of a major TV show, but it soon became clear that we were completely incompatible. Mr Producer had been to a wrap party the night before, had had two vodkas, and was freaked out by his over-indulgence. He then refused to eat anything straight off the menu, instead everything had to be gluten/sugar/fat/fun free, and heaven forbid if the dressing was anything other than on the side. We did not make it to any base; if I wanted to witness a lunchtime temper tantrum I would have opted for visiting a toddler-toting friend of mine.

Another good indicator of skilled prowess in the bedroom is dancing. A man who is a good dancer, taking the lead in a firm, but gentle, oh-so-sexy way, is universally acknowledged to, well, simply shag you senseless in superior fashion.

The date is going really well if neither of you looks at your mobile. If you spend the evening replying to all the friends you have arranged to text you so you look popular, give up and go find Bunbury. If he does instead, or as well, give up and go find Bunbury.

It is traditional for a man to pay during these early stages; however, you are a modern woman, so always offer – even if you do not expect to actually fork out. If you are on later dinner dates with a man who is more financially stretched than you, it may be tactful to go to the loo and subtly pay en route, or if he leaves the table, take the opportunity to deal with the bill then. This ensures he loses no face – he can jokingly complain that you have paid, whilst being slightly relieved that he does not have to face the potential indignity of his over-the-limit credit card being refused.

The last hurdle of the date to get over is goodbye. I am trying to train an SG friend who thinks that it is impolite not to kiss someone if they have taken her out, that it is actually ruder to snog them and never speak to them again. If you do not want to kiss them, you will need to think on your feet and take control of the situation as you say farewell, firmly giving them a quick peck on the cheek before swiftly departing. If you linger, they can lunge. You may find it helpful to invest in a security light for your front door. Not only can they scare off burglars; they may frighten away Objects you do not want to kiss. An SG friend installed one outside her door and 'forgets' to inform any date she does not want to kiss about the impending illumination. Whilst he does dazed-rabbit-caught-in-the-headlights, she has just enough time to rush inside alone and go play with a more appealing kind of rabbit.

A man's behaviour at the end of the date says so much – some may take chivalry to a new level. One Distraction I was unsure of earned a second date because when I got into a taxi he handed over a crisp £20 note to the driver and told him to make sure I got home safely. It was not about the money; simply that no (straight) man had ever behaved so gallantly with me before. I told my brother the tale and he said he constantly made the same gesture – no wonder he is always attached. The birth of the modern independent woman does not mean society should suffer the death of old-fashioned manners.

Post-date

There are two scenarios after the date. Either you want another one (or are in two minds about him so you think he has earned a second hearing to help you reach your verdict), or you do not.

If you have decided the Distraction is not for you after all, it is easier. Ditching is covered in more detail in the following chapter, but at this early stage probably all you need do is text him 'thank you' at the end of the evening, then do not contact him. If he phones your mobile from his, do not answer, and if he calls you from an unidentified number and you accidentally pick up, tell him he has got you 'at a bad time' or you are 'in a meeting'. Then, do not return his call and instead leave it a few days before e-mailing or texting him in response to anything he has asked you, but including no questions yourself, and making clear that you are utterly manic for the foreseeable future. You have thus kept it polite, but a clear no-go. You do not necessarily want to alienate a new friend – his circle could be packed full with other potential Objects that you would like to distract yourself with.

If you want another date, do not text him 'thank you' at the end of the evening, since then you are prematurely playing all your cards. By waiting, you will have left yourself the option of texting or e-mailing him 'thank you' first thing the following morning – it is only polite, after all. By leaving the expression of your gratitude to the following day, you create the opportunity for banter and have made it easier for him to suggest another encounter.

If you want this particular Distraction, remember the following truth, uttered by one of London's most eligible bachelors (mothers and fathers positively unlock their daughters as far as he is concerned): if a man wants to be with you, he will find you. Post-date, follow the golden rule that passive is active. Bombarding him with missives is not cool – if you want him you must hold your nerve. Yes, (very) bitter personal experience popping up again. And remember, if he is really serious it could take him a few days to ask you out again. One SG friend recently had to wait almost a week for her Distraction to get back in touch after what she thought was a phenomenal date. It turns out it was so good that he got scared and had to decide whether he really did want a girlfriend or not, then dropped his phone down the loo and spent several more days trying to track down her number (heroically withstanding the consequent mass mickey-taking by everyone he contacted – and the mutual friends they in turn told).

Occasionally you may bypass the date stage and just go directly to the kissing one. If you want the act to be a repeat occurrence and you kissed him the night before in a random non-date situation, such as a clinch in a club's corner, you are not allowed to contact him the following day. IT WILL GET YOU NOWHERE; I am backed up on this one by every SG who contributed to the research for this book. The day after the kiss, the ball is in his court – you are not about to lower yourself to carrying out the chasing chore, leave it to him.

You may still at this time have more than one ball in play. There are some advantages to dual or even triple dating – the less you care, the more aloof you are; the more aloof you are, the more likely a man is to find you attractive since he will have to chase you. In New York it is perfectly acceptable to be dating a number of men, but less so in the UK, where we are still slightly less mercenary about the process. One New Yorker SG I know actually asks a man how much they earn before she even agrees to a date, and the men are so used to this behaviour that they tell her without hesitation. Not so in the UK of course, where any mention of money is considered acceptable strictly in WAG-wannabe domain.

The golden rule when it comes to the number of Distractions you are juggling is that if you are having problems justifying it to yourself, there is a problem. And if you have got to the exchanging bodily fluid stage, you may be getting an SG reputation you do not want when more than one man is involved.

If you are dating a foreigner, do keep in mind that things can get lust in translation. My Hollywood Distraction texted me asking me to 'hook-up', which I instantly, and rather over-excitedly, took as an obscene invitation, before an American Platonic Boyfriend of mine explained that to him the term would have altogether more innocent connotations.

Kissing

We now turn to the exchange of bodily fluids with your Distractions, the delicious naughtiness that may be an outcome of any of the scenarios described above. Again, keep in mind that this is supposed to be the really fun part of dating. If it is not, serious re-consideration of your involvement with the Distraction is in order.

The terms kiss or **kiss and cuddle** have become polite euphemisms often used to refer to anything from a slight snog to full-on sex. In terms of kissing in traditional forms, if he is a bad kisser and a nice person, it may be tricky. There are some men who can be taught, but if he is really awful at first base he is probably going to be dreadful at anything past it. I learnt this the hard way. One man was not only the worst kisser in the world, he was so bad in bed it was lucky he did not put me off sex for life; he just put me off blonde men. I now exclusively date dark, swarthy types because the experience was so unpleasant, although perhaps one day I will find a blonde Adonis (MySpace-message me if you have Daniel Craig's mobile) to cure me of my phobia.

You may be an SG with the ability to separate sex from emotion, in which case, go play. However, if you prefer your sex spiced with a little meaning then that is something to be celebrated too – it seems to be a biological fact of life that there are fewer guys than dolls of this persuasion. However much I and my girlfriends wish we could, and although this may mean we have to depend on other methods of satisfaction at times (masturbation is the thinking (wo)man's television set after all), we cannot have sex without feelings getting involved. If a man is unable to bring himself to call a girl his girlfriend, we are simply unable to shag him without it all ending in tears, and it is never his waterworks that get taxed.

Whatever the case, old stereotypes do, to an extent, die hard. If you want to keep the dating power, do not have sex with a man until you have him where you want him. You can do everything else, but all my Platonic Boyfriends confirm that the act itself always makes the difference – once you have slept with someone you can never go back, and men, unless their minds are already hooked on you, may not want to go forward. The aforementioned eligible bachelor only ever tries for a rerun with girls who would not go all the way with him the first time they had got it on. He freely admits that if they had succumbed, he would not bother.

Some Platonic Boyfriends of mine think it is a marvellous idea to have f**k buddies – girls they have no strings sex with to alleviate physical frustration. You are an SG, thus well within your rights to have a lover whose sole purpose is to relieve any sexual pangs you might have. However, I have yet to find an SG who has had this arrangement and found that it works for them, although I naturally have several Platonic Boyfriends who do. In official statistics, men say they have slept with more women than women say they have with men. Which means that either the men are exaggerating, the women are being modest, or, for some unearthly reason, everyone is being economical with the truth. Whatever the case, the males that I know do accept that their f**k buddies are not platonic girlfriends.

By definition, to have a real platonic relationship, you should not kiss each other. If you suspect that hormones might take over in a Platonic Boyfriend's company, it may be necessary to maintain distance or always have someone else with you in his presence for a little while, just to make sure there is no heat of the moment you both could get carried away in. The reason why I have so many

Platonic Boyfriends is that we have not had so much as an Eskimo kiss. If you think you may want to get naked with them, you must accept that once those boundaries are passed your relationship will never be the same, although friendship can probably survive a slight snog as long as it is of the humorous variety. I was once standing at a cocktail party holding court with three gay men; we then discovered we had all kissed the same man, who we all still consider as a Platonic Boyfriend. Bisexuality is probably something we should all consider more carefully – it makes everything an option, and as SGs we are about not having ours limited. Several female friends of mine have tried and enjoyed girls. One sexually ambiguous SG reports that it is always sensible for your first experiences to be with someone who knows what they are doing, and she now organises visits to all-girl parties for her more curious SG friends.

There is a distinct possibility that since you spend most of your time at work you may get involved with someone from that environment. It is inevitable that everyone there will immediately find out, but just try to keep your behaviour as discriminating as possible so you can at least function in your professional capacity. This means no naughty nookie on site. One friend had her distinctive diamante encrusted hold-ups discovered by a director, hanging over the back of his chair at the beginning of a breakfast meeting in the boardroom; she had left them there after a moment of passion the night before with one of her male trainees. This was not her finest hour. Fortunately, no one could take any serious action against her; my friend had made it her business to know precisely how many of the directors were kissing their PAs.

These directors were almost all married. As touched on in the selection process, please try not to get entangled with attached people. Those SGs who have affairs with the boss and married men give us all a bad name, which makes managing our worlds all the harder, as it just adds fuel to the fire of attached women's wary perception of us.

Turning to more traditional methods of dating, when is the right time for sex with someone you are 'exclusive' with? General SG consensus, garnered from the accurate method of putting together a focus group of females and feeding them vodka whilst playing Madonna's greatest hits, seems to point to the fifth date rule being positively virginal, with the third a more realistic scenario. Standard methods to prevent clothes removal before then is to limit alcohol intake and time spent alone with him at yours/his, and not get a bikini wax or shave your legs. However, I do know of one SG who has been known to shave her legs mid-date.

Try not to get hung up about what you perceive to be your body's shortcomings. Not only will he probably not have noticed before you draw attention to them; such anxiety is not alluring to a man, whilst your physical person almost certainly will be. Men get excited about breasts, full stop – they do not have them (if your Distraction does, either ditch or diet him) so by biological twist of fate are fascinated by them. Your Object will also be too busy worrying about his performance to be concerned with your slightly squidgy belly. Do not fear cellulite or wrinkles – so many attractive men I know find women over 30 sexier than their younger counterparts – they know what they are doing in the bedroom and have far fewer inhibitions. Allow age to bring confidence in one's own skin, and that is attractive. Thank God.

The older you are, the less shocked you will probably be if some sexual boundary pushing is proposed, and indeed you probably find the prospect so tantalising that you bring it up yourself. Of course you have to remain within some sort of comfort zone, but there are always varying degrees of naughtiness that you can compromise on. One friend's Distraction loved the idea of handcuffs; the metal variety did nothing for her, but the pink fluffy ones were an orgasmic compromise. However, do keep hold of the handcuff key; one SG friend lost hers whilst indulging in some solo action (do not ask), and her flatmate had to help her out of her predicament. Fortunately it was her female one who found her, as her male one would probably have joined in.

Some men are turned on massively by anal sex (which is why they often have a fetish for French women – apparently they are much more open to it); however, if you are not, suggest other routes in for the pair of you – you into him, for instance. He will either run a mile and not bring the topic up again, or you get a pain-free solution.

People are prone to finding the most extraordinary things a turn-on, so do not be afraid of talking through your fantasies; they are probably quite pedestrian. I was once in the immigration queue at JFK Airport in New York and got chatted up by a film producer. The line was lengthy, and it turned out we were both going to the same S&M-themed Halloween party and had done a tour of the same Soho sex shops back in London. As liberated single people we thought we had seen it all, but still managed to out-shock one another with our outrageous discoveries. (And almost all the immigration queue as well – although a retired couple seemed to be nodding in a manner that implied they had seen/done it all before, or maybe it was just jetlag.)

Accidental Sex

Of course, sex does not only happen in a relationship. You are an SG, and unless you are of iron will, you will occasionally have AS. Boys tend to have one-night stands, whereas girls have AS (an SG rarely intends at the outset that the situation would go as far as it did or believes such a liaison is going to happen only the once).

Do not beat yourself up or feel guilty about AS; you had fun, you wanted to do it at the time, so be it. Almost every SG has done the same, they may just not admit to it. Safe sex is advisable, but might not always happen; you are a grown-up and can get thee to a pharmacist or doctor and deal with it, even if you are suffering from the hangover from hell.

Relationships rarely tend to come out of AS encounters. Therefore try not to mess up and have AS with someone you really like. I know it is hard, but irritatingly it is all about the chase for a boy, and once you have AS with him, he has already won the prize. Invariably, the only way he will want a repeat performance with you is if you convince yourself that he will never return, and move on. If a man sees you functioning fabulously without him, his interest may be piqued again.

In the long term, AS with someone you never have to see again is far easier to deal with than with someone you do, although there is potential for major misjudgement this way. One SG awoke to find a very attractive, but anxious man in her bed. When she asked him what the problem was, he said he needed his medication. For multiple personality disorder. It took two Platonic Boyfriends and her GBF's shitsu (the GBF helpfully got scared so went and waited for them in the nearest cocktail lounge) to eject him when his second personality declared squatter's rights. I jest not.

However, the act is more likely to be with someone that you know, invariably a co-worker or Platonic Boyfriend. If it is the former, never, ever have an exchange regarding the AS at work; you do not want to run the risk of being overheard or having a missive forwarded and damaging your career. Keep your poise around him at all times for the respect to return. If the AS is with a Platonic Boyfriend, unless both of you suddenly realise that you want to try and make an official go of things, then you have messed up. It will take months to get back on track, if ever. Sorry.

Sunrise is not as flattering as sunset, and if it is an AS situation you are rousing from, is probably especially true in all its hung-over glory. You really should not be waking up in his bed, as you should have known better and enticed him back to yours; however, accidents do happen. Thus if you awake at your Distraction's, and it is possible workwise, aim for either the extremely early getaway or mid-morning departure, when there are fewer people about. If you can afford it, then order a cabbage, but not a firm who knows you and your family well (one SG's father was informed by the local taxi driver of her post-coital movements), and never utilise work's taxi account. An SG friend did this and although her female boss signed it off, she was sharp enough to notice the extraneous expense and it was brought up at the Office Christmas Party.

There will not be that much you can do about your Dusty Springfield impression if waking in the Distraction's abode and he has no female housemates. However, you can deal with any major mascara issues by using his Vaseline and a tissue. These items will be located somewhere near his bed; best not to ask why. If you have to get through the office or family party without having been home, take a shower at his, use any of his products and then just brazen it out. Boots can open fairly early, whilst one SG who has a 10 a.m. start at work sometimes pops by Topshop en route. Another SG who was having a playing hard phase found it prudent to keep a spare top in her desk at work just in case of any emergencies – if anyone else saw it she claimed that it was there because she lived in fear of spilling something down her shirt. She is such a messy eater it was eminently believable.

If you have managed to be somewhat sensible and the interlude took place at your abode, you may have to deal with turfing the Object out. Start noisily getting ready for work; he should soon get the message as you waft toothpaste at him.

At this moment of the morning, if you have had AS and are hoping beyond all reason that he will contact you after and he does not already have your number, you need to give it to him. There is a slightly subtler option to this awkward exchange; pretend you cannot find your mobile and get him to call it from his so yours rings. Lo and behold, he has your number, and you his, but please leave it to him to contact you. You must expect that he will probably not.

The other and hottest form of AS, is, of course ex-sex. Emotionally, it is almost always a head f**k of highest proportions, although physically there is nothing so blissful or so naughty as rediscovering the body of someone you used to date, and probably should be nowhere near. You know each other's sexual buttons and the frisson of kissing someone you thought you never would again is almost always mind-blowing. Unless they were useless in bed to begin with of course, when it is just a useful reminder of why you are no longer with him. Numerous SG friends have ex-sex stories, but nothing tops the situation one sexually empowered SG friend of mine found herself in. I called her up as her ex had been on Breakfast TV as the 'expert' on some subject... My SG had seen it, having watched him on the box whilst in bed with another ex. Both of them were involved in a begging war to have her back; the main reason for their desire, of course, was that she was determined to keep them ex. Being an SG made her happier than being with either of them – and on this note, we turn to the final chapter of our SG celebration.

Chapter Nine

Survival of the SG Fittest

Long-term boyfriend management, how to truly nurture and maintain a relationship, is a whole different book, so in this final chapter we discuss extraction and methods of disentangling ourselves from unsuitable liaisons.

In the early encounters of dating and kissing, any relationship with a Distraction will likely be an ambiguous one, where neither of you will be entirely sure of where you stand. However, there will come a moment when either you or your Distraction get so dissatisfied by the vague situation that you require some definition. The time has come when you either regain official full-blown SG status or lose it to become an **Attached Girl** (AG).

Many of us tend to be averse to direct confrontation in such matters close to the heart. Typically, the female is anxious to avoid accusations of getting ahead of herself, whilst the male will only reluctantly admit their taming. So, if you do suffer a sudden bout of shyness about baring your soul despite already having bared all, it may well be that you receive clarification on your relationship by a third party. I once attended a soirée with an Object and someone asked him, in my presence, if I was his girlfriend. He appeared aghast, but being a well brought-up boy he mumbled that yes, I was, 'absolutely'. His consummate impression of a trapped mouse made me instantly steel myself to the inevitable and, sure enough, later that night Mickey did indeed settle the situation in private... by officially ditching me. There are of course alternative endings – many an SG I know has discovered that she was someone's girlfriend because he introduced her as such. Sometimes the surprise has even been a pleasant one.

Of course, it should be different, and in an ideal world if you find yourself falling for your Distraction he should be shouting to all and sundry that he loves you more than football etc. etc... However, in this commitment-free, easy-refund world, my SG friends and I have found that for an increasing number of men, actually granting the title 'girlfriend' is a huge deal.

You may find that the Distraction in question requires a little nudging/management to make the status official. A reliable tactic so many of my AG friends have used is to turn on the serious charm with their Object's family and friends (although with the male ones, not to the extent that it could be construed as flirting). This results in his nearest and dearest deciding that the girl is 'a good thing', and they start referring to her as his girlfriend. If everyone around your Distraction has accorded you this status, especially if you meet his parents (usual drill: appropriate dress, CL etc.) he is likely just to go along with it.

Either way, the ambiguous relationship ends in one of two outcomes – commitment or ditching (when you are either the ditcher or ditchee).

Commitment

Actually having a boyfriend is a massive culture shock for the SG – slightly selfish to somewhat selfless is a gigantic leap. If you are going into a relationship, keep sight of the fact that your SG feistiness is what attracted him to you in the first place. Any unreasonable behaviour on his part should be swiftly countered – so if he demands you have that Brazilian, you are within your rights to insist he has a back wax. Fair's fair in love and ingrown hairs.

You know that being an SG can be fabulously fun, but so can being with someone if it works. Men are wonderful when the situation is right, but the unhappiness they can bring also knows no bounds. If he is not good for your heart, self and soul, ditch him.

The Ditch

Ditcher

Although people often declare that a split is a mutual decision, we all know that, in reality, there is normally a ditcher and a ditchee.

If your relationship is particularly ambiguous and you wish to just let it die a natural death, you may not need to take any direct action at all. If you can just gently drift out of kissing each other rather than cause unnecessary embarrassment on either side, do so. Keep in mind that boys have a tendency to think about the ramifications of romantic encounters rather less than girls, so they may not rate the relationship as much as you do anyway. Several Platonic Boyfriends of mine have been dumped by girls they did not realise they were going out with, much to their bemusement and amusement, so there may well be a good chance that no action need be taken.

This is the only time it is acceptable to ditch someone by the silent treatment – otherwise ensure your behaviour is better suited to the adult arena than the playground. The love of my life's last words to me were 'see you soon'; he then failed to contact me again, or return any of my attempts to get in touch with him, and his behaviour was the catalyst for my nervous breakdown. There was obviously something special enough for you to be with your Distraction, thus give him the respect he deserves and end it properly.

A word of warning, however, before you do the deed. Fools rush in to a relationship, but they also rush out. It is only natural if you sometimes have panic attacks about whether you want to have a boyfriend at all, since after perfecting the art of the SG party you must now learn the AG art of the compromise. However, being an AG is not necessarily worse, just different, so if you are having doubts do not run from him in haste. Whatever your distaste over his unsavoury habits, scratching and rearranging himself at every opportunity may not necessarily be a directly ditchable offence, unless he does it in front of your mother.

There are times, of course, when it is vital you jettison the attachment. A friend of mine was working in a high-pressure job in a television newsroom, where the computer systems kept going down on a regular basis. She made friends with the IT guy – he did not look like your standard technical geek, but appeared normal, if American. At first, the relationship was fantastic – she had never been with someone who was so sensitive, who seemed to understand her so well. When she needed him to be keen, he was. When she required him to take a step back, he did. Her friends loved him – he remembered their names, their backgrounds. And then newsroom girl realised; the IT guy was reading her e-mail. This is stalking. If a man's behaviour to you – or indeed yours to him – ever degenerates into the same realm (sneaking a peek at a phone to read text messages, check the call register...), showing him or yourself the virtual door is probably the only option.

If you ditch, mind your manners. No need to sink as low as those litmus tests of disagreeable taste, Britney and KFed, and declare divorce by text. E-mail is slightly less dreadful, but a phone or even a face-to-face conversation is preferable and most proper. Gently explain that it is not working for you, but you had a great time, and get out.

Sometimes the Distraction might refuse to accept the concept that you just do not want to be with him and will keep attempting to remain in your world. Once this has progressed to a ridiculous level you may need to be mildly impolite, but there is no need to be exceptionally rude and just ignore them. They are human after all, and will eventually get the message even if it is by accident rather than design. One SG friend dumped a man who just would not take no for an answer, and was so inundated with presents, flowers and balloons from him that she started to distribute them amongst her friends. Irritatingly I was late on the uptake, and all that was left by the time I got to her goodies was a balloon in the shape of a dolphin. I was subsequently spotted by her ex, bestowing a young boy with the present at the bus stop because the child found it so hysterical. On registering the ex's stricken face I informed my SG friend she probably would not be hearing from him again – and so it proved.

Ditchee

Rejection is something we all have to deal with at some point, but being rebuffed is never easy. There are, however, certain procedures to employ to make the process of being the ditchee slightly less painful.

Once he has told you that it is over, if he does it in person or on the phone, quietly accept what he has said then do your best to get away so you can keep as much of your self-respect as possible. If it is by e-mail, wait at least 24 hours and get your friends to check your reply before you send it. Things said in the height of passion rarely look good in the cold light of day. We have all done it – one friend had a hissy fit and tipped a glass of wine over her partner at a restaurant before storming out – only to have to creep back in to a round of applause from their fellow diners to beg him to hand over her keys. Furious about the red wine stain ruining his adored vintage army jacket and his humiliation in front of a maître d' he had spent years tipping to secure special service, the man dropped them into her soup before striding out, never to speak to her again – and leaving her to pick up the bill. Bunny boiler behaviour is never endearing.

When you have removed yourself from his vicinity, immediately allocate him the same ring/message tone on your mobile as all other previous disappointments; the **Promise Much, Deliver Little (PMDL)** boys. The PMDLs are a selection of scoundrels who bruise egos or even break hearts. For this PMDL group, I advise assigning them all the same, most ridiculous noise option your phone has to offer (ducks quacking, for instance), so if he should ever get in touch, the sounds emitting from your phone will send you into tears of mirth rather than despair. The fact that there is more than one man on this list reduces their consequence to a very weak blip on your radar and serves to put everything into perspective – you have been here before, you have survived, there will be other Objects. Edit his name in your phone to a good reason not to contact him. For example, you could rename him 'I'm bad news' or 'Git'. Be warned, however. A particularly organised SG friend of mine synchronised all her mobile phone contacts with her e-mail ones, and then sent out an automatically generated e-mail to everyone in her address book with all the details she had for them, asking the recipients to check and update them if required. Unfortunately, this meant that 'Small

Penis' and her other PMDLs to whom she had given similar monikers all saw the nicknames she had allocated them. Not perhaps her life's most magical moment.

For the sake of your sanity, it is essential to retain perspective and not to place him on a pedestal of perfection where he does not warrant such a position. His absence should not be allowed to make your heart grow fonder – however convinced you are it was a match made in heaven, heaven has decided it is not. There is no point daydreaming endless scenarios where he tracks you down to Dixons and declares his undying love amongst the video cameras so the incident is relayed on all the television sets in the shop window in climatic Richard Curtis rom-com fashion. Anything other than ex-sex rarely works, and that only lasts as long as the orgasm(s).

If an Object splits up with you, try not to hit the Internet or harass mutual friends to find out what and who he is up to and, if the opportunity arises, abstain from checking his e-mail or his phone. A man with a touch of the playboy about him was in the process of ditching a close friend of mine. He regularly checked his e-mail from her home computer and often forgot to logout, and once, in desperate state, she stole a sly glance at it. This was an error. She could have done without knowing the specifics of his porn order or the several SGs of her acquaintance bemoaning their AS with him. It also proved to be a fashion disaster for her – she found eye contact with these girls and him awkward for months after, so was forced to wear huge bug-eyed shades out and about, garnering herself the unfortunate nickname, 'Bono'.

There will always be something positive you can take from the experience – **EXploitation** if you will. My friends and I now have a running joke that we take from each ex a 'use', that will stay with us for years to come; the more inane, the greater the entertainment derived. One man shifted my television set 20 degrees to the right and it has enhanced my viewing pleasure every time I switch my TV on, whilst an SG friend took this a step further, and actually groomed her unfaithful boyfriend for his use before they split. He had a touch of the Jamie Olivers about him so she got him to teach her how to make the most delicious chocolate fondant puddings (one with runny warm gooey chocolate inside).

Implement, as far as you can, a policy whereby you try never to fall out with an ex. I do have one Genuine Girlfriend who has the sophisticated method of only dating people from a certain London area, miles from her abode, thus limiting the likely chance of seeing her exes to when she is visiting her new man for sex, but she is not normal. For the rest of us, we are liable to run into them from time to time. It is not easy if you are single and the ex is with someone new, but an occupational hazard of being out is that you will bump into him – out is where you probably met after all. A friend of mine sagely says that the only time it is acceptable to run into an ex-boyfriend is when you are in black tie dress and on the arm of a more good-looking and visibly successful man, whilst he has just left the gym. Unfortunately, life does not always work out that way. However, you are a happy SG, in tune with your body beautiful, so even if you do collide with them returning from your workout – and this has happened to me – it is whilst you are wearing very cute gym gear. Does it really matter? They will have perfect recall of you in more compromising positions.

With determination, you will find a balanced state of mind about love affairs going awry. However horrible it is, you deal. There is a reason why you are not together, whether it be his blindness to how incredible you are, timing, distance... Do not let him make you hide away; he has caused you enough distress already. One of my SG friends, when dealing with a relationship gone wrong, tries to take what she can learn from it and then look at her situation like pressing the 'new game' button on a computer game. You get to move on, to start again, and with what you have learnt will hopefully fare better on the next attempt... whilst scoring more frequently.

The End?

We finish our SG journey with a glass-raising tribute to the SG in all her splendiferous glory.

So you are single? Your life is not over, it has only just begun. You are keeping your options open until worthy ones come along, and that is absolutely the right decision to make. According to official statistics, it is men rather than women who are more likely to be single – if you do want a Distraction, the odds are in your favour. Today's world has bequeathed to the SG the gift of time – it is no longer the enemy of the SG it once was, but is on your side, so panic not. The average age of brides and mothers is ever increasing, society realising that it is healthier to have fulfilled, confident women rocking and ruling the cradle and the world.

There is no right or wrong path – and we SGs are lucky, as others have already blazed a trail for us, whether it be doing a Madonna and marrying a toy boy late in life, or opting for the Elizabeth I route and avoiding matrimony altogether, instead courting and trailing admirers in your wake. We have the chance to enjoy the fruits of their pioneering, so do so. There is nothing to fear about being single, instead it is a lifestyle that can be celebrated with friends, family – and fabulous footwear. All this book says is that you deserve to indulge yourself, to be comfortable within your own skin and with your own company – and the people in your world will appreciate the knock-on effect since the happiness radiating from you will be infectious.

A single girl is undoubtedly in possession of a good fortune, as she has the freedom to lead the life she wants – all it takes is a little management.

www.summersdale.com